The Complete Make-a-Mix Cookbook

How to Make Your Own Mixes

*by Karine Eliason, Nevada Harward
and Madeline Westover*

HPBooks
a division of
PRICE STERN SLOAN
Los Angeles

© 1990 by HPBooks

Published by HPBooks, a division of Price Stern Sloan, Inc.
Los Angeles, California
Printed in the U.S.A.
9 8 7 6 5 4 3 2 1

Library of Congress Cataloging-in-Publication Data

Eliason, Karine.
    The complete make-a-mix cookbook/by Karine Eliason, Nevada
Harward and Madeline Westover.
      p. cm
    Includes index.
    ISBN 1-55788-013-1
    1. Food mixes. I. Harward, Nevada. II. Westover, Madeline.
III. Title.
TX652.E369 1991
641.5'5—dc20
                                                  90-44145
                                                     CIP

This book has been printed on acid-free paper.

Cover photography by Teri Sandison, Los Angeles.

Cover food styling by Norman Stewart.

Some accessories used for cover photography are courtesy of *Bullock's* and *Tessoro*.

Front cover photo, clockwise from top: Giant Braided Loaf, page 141, Crunchy Granola Mix, page 41, Deep-Dish Pot Pie, page 111, Fresh Peach Pie, page 165, Slice and Bake Oatmeal Cookies, page 47, Old-Fashioned Vegetable Platter, page 72, and Best-Ever Minestrone Soup, page 62.

Back cover photo: Golden Cornbread, page 131 and Dinner-in-a-Pumpkin, page 101.

Contents

Baking and Cooking with Mixes

The Magic of Mixes

One quick look at your cupboard shelves will tell you that mixes have become an essential part of today's cooking. Our busy life-style has created a major trend toward the use of time-saving convenience foods and mixes are the popular choice for many of our cooking needs. Because the time-consuming part of cooking is assembling supplies and equipment and measuring ingredients, it's easy to see why mixes are so valuable to every cook.

Mixes Are Easy

With your own mixes, you can save almost three-fourths the time you spend preparing food items. This is possible because you prepare for several meals at one time. Whether your family has 2 or 22 members, you can make just the right amount for each meal. The results are better planned, more delicious and more nutritious even when time is at a minimum. Most recipes from mixes are so easy your children can learn to make them.

Mixes Are Economical

Although commercial mixes provide convenience, they are generally advertised as time-savers rather than money-savers. Their prices increase regularly with rising labor and packaging costs. Why not save those extra dollars by providing the labor and packaging yourself? Compare the cost per cup of commercial mixes with homemade mixes and you'll discover your mixes cost less than half the price of store mixes. You can save even more by watching for specials on staple items such as flour, sugar and shortening.

Mixes Are Nutritious

There's a special satisfaction in choosing your own ingredients to cook with, and knowing what is in your foods. If you want to reduce the amount of preservatives and additives you consume, making your own mixes is the way to start. Commercial mixes are, of necessity, prepared for a long shelf life. Food values may decrease with time and it is often impossible to know just how old a product is at the time you purchase it. Some packaged mixes may be over a year old.

When you make meals from your own mixes, you'll notice the fresher flavor. The mix recipes in this book contain ingredients chosen for their health value.

Mixes Are Versatile

The variety and extent to which mixes can be used is almost limitless. Perhaps, you prefer a multi-purpose mix such as QUICK MIX, which makes dozens of different recipes. It can be substituted for any recipe that calls for the commercially prepared biscuit mixes.

You can choose, according to the type of storage space available to you, whether you want to prepare BASIC COOKIE MIX, a dry mix which stores on your pantry shelf, or any of the SLICE AND BAKE COOKIES that require freezer storage. Both can be used to make a variety of cookies.

Pies are quick and easy when you keep FREEZER PIE CRUST MIX on hand. And don't forget that main dishes come from mixes, too. Try our favorite MEXICAN MEAT MIX that can be used to make a variety of Mexican dishes. The CHICKEN MIX is a great one to keep around to provide a head start for all those recipes that require two cups of cooked chicken. You save freezer space as well, with the deboned chicken meat, which is another plus for the CHICKEN MIX. With a few basic meat mixes, you can provide your family with a large assortment of quick, nutritious meals.

Some mixes are seasonings to complement specific recipes. Make individual packets of TACO SEASONING MIX, HOME-STYLE DRESSING MIX, ITALIAN-STYLE MEAT SAUCE MIX and the other various "special" mixes and you're ready for any occasion! You'll find they're better than those you can buy. Some are so unique you can't even buy them in stores.

Nevada Harward, Madeline Westover and Karine Eliason

The Ingredients

When you're making your own mixes, you'll want to use the best ingredients you can get, because foods you prepare are only as good as their contents. Always use fresh, high-quality products.

It's important to know what each ingredient offers to a recipe. This gives you the confidence to guarantee success every time in the kitchen. Here are some tips to help you make mixes and meals everyone will remember.

Flours

All-purpose flour is best in most dry mixes. It is a blend of hard and soft wheat flours. Bleached or unbleached flour can be used alternately, but unbleached flour has a higher nutritional value. As moisture varies in wheat flours, some yeast bread recipes indicate an approximate measurement. Always begin with a small amount of flour and add more until the desired texture is reached.

Whole-wheat flour can be used interchangeably with all-purpose flour by using 1 to 2 tablespoons less per cup of flour called for. When using whole-wheat flour, the leavening needs to be increased (yeast almost doubled, baking powder and baking soda increased by one-third). Mixes made with whole-wheat flour should be refrigerated to retain maximum nutrition.

Fats

Butter and margarine are used interchangeably in most recipes. However, butter produces a somewhat different texture and flavor than margarine and should be used in those recipes where specified. Butter and margarine are both perishable and mixes containing either should be refrigerated.

Vegetable oils are pressed from seeds, fruits and nuts. These are more versatile and more easily available than other liquid fats.

Hydrogenated vegetable shortening is preferred in most recipes. Mixes containing vegetable shortening may be covered and stored in a cool, dry place for 3 months or more.

Eggs

Fresh eggs are a boost to every recipe because they have a much better texture and taste than eggs that have been stored awhile. Use large eggs, about 2 ounces in weight. Eggs at room temperature produce more volume.

Leavening Agents

Active dry yeast is convenient for mixing purposes. Yeast is comprised of living organisms that feed on sugars and produce alcohol and carbon dioxide. Be certain the liquid you add to the yeast is lukewarm, about 105 to 110F.

Baking powder generally starts to work when it is combined with liquid, but its principal impact on a product is increased when the product is heated. Double-acting baking powder is preferred for its availability and consistency.

Baking soda alone has no leavening properties, but when used in combination with acid ingredients such as sour milk or molasses, it produces a tender crumb texture.

Sugar

Sugars contribute sweetness and tenderness to foods. In breads, sugar aids in producing a golden brown crust. Small pinches of sugar added to certain vegetables increase their flavor. Granulated sugar is usually used in these recipes. Use powdered sugar, brown sugar, honey and molasses only when specified. They are not interchangeable with granulated sugar.

Spices

Sometimes the difference between an outstanding and a mediocre dish is the seasoning added. Our recipes allow you to use a wide variety of herbs, seasonings and spices. For best results, use recently purchased, high-quality spices, because spices tend to lose their flavor in a short time.

Vegetables, Meats and Poultry

The greatest care should be used in preparing vegetables, meats and poultry for storage. It is essential to use fresh, clean, top-quality ingredients. Follow directions carefully for preparing, freezing and storing frozen mixes.

Instant Nonfat Dry Milk

With milk solids added to a dry mix, you have the option of adding water to the recipe instead of milk. Adding milk gives extra enrichment and nutrition.

Master Mixes, clockwise from lower left: Herbed Stuffing, page 17, Wheat Mix, page 14, Basic Mix, page 19, Crunchy Granola Mix, page 41, Quick Mix, page 11, Brownie Mix, page 19

Equipment and Procedures

On the whole *The Complete Make-a-Mix Cookbook* is very similar to the way you cook now. You probably already have all the equipment you need for measuring, mixing and storing the ingredients.

The procedures for combining ingredients will be slightly different than cooking "from scratch." You will spend a little extra time preparing your mixes, but you'll save much more time in the final preparation of recipes. Make up several mixes at a time. Because you're working mainly with dry ingredients, the clean-up will be minimal. In just a short time, you can fill your shelves with an abundance of mixes that will make cooking more enjoyable for weeks to come.

Measuring

Accuracy in measuring ingredients is necessary to insure satisfactory results in your cooking. You should have:

- a set of dry measuring cups
- a liquid measuring cup with pouring spout
- a set of measuring spoons
- a straight-edged spatula
- a rubber scraper

Dry Ingredients should be measured in a cup with a flush rim for leveling. Lightly spoon ingredients into a cup and level with a straight-edged spatula.

1. These basic kitchen utensils are all you need for making mixes. A pastry blender makes it easier to cut shortening into dry ingredients.

2. Lots of airtight canisters, jars and cans are useful for storing mixes. Freezer containers should allow for expansion of frozen mixes.

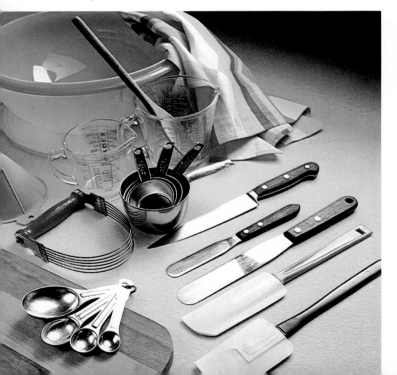

Liquid Ingredients require a transparent measuring cup with markings and a pouring spout. Measure liquid ingredients at eye-level.

Moist Ingredients such as brown sugar, soft bread crumbs, grated cheese, coconut or raisins should be firmly packed so they hold the shape of the cup when turned out.

Solid Ingredients such as vegetable shortening should be pressed firmly into the measuring cup or spoon so no air pockets remain. Level with a straight-edged spatula. Use a rubber scraper to get all the shortening out of the measure.

Mixing

A real convenience in preparing mixes is a heavy-duty mixer. A small electric mixer or pastry blender will produce the same results but require more effort. If you do not have a pastry blender, you can use 2 knives to evenly distribute dry ingredients and fats.

You will definitely need an extra-large mixing bowl to combine mixes. If you do not have a bowl large enough to hold about 35 cups (9 quarts) of mix, a round-bottom dishpan is an alternative.

For dry mixes, the usual procedure is to combine all dry ingredients until evenly distributed, then cut in vegetable shortening, butter or margarine until the mixture resembles cornmeal in texture.

3. Store seasoning mixes in aluminum foil packets folded and wrapped tightly to keep out air.

4. On each mix container write the name of the mix and the date by which it should be used. If you wish, also record the amount of mix and recipe page number.

Storing

For maximum freshness, the best way to store your mixes is in airtight containers placed in a cool, dry and dark place. Mixes to be stored in the freezer must be put in containers allowing for at least 1/2-inch expansion. Lightweight plastic bags and cottage cheese cartons are not suitable for freezer use. Your frozen mixes should be thawed in the refrigerator or microwave oven, and used immediately after thawing.

You will want to consider two methods of storing dry mixes, depending on your needs: Large Canister Storage or Premeasured Storage.

Large Canister Storage lets you store your mixes in one or several large containers. This is especially useful for QUICK MIX, HOT ROLL MIX and other mixes that make a large number of recipes. You can use large coffee cans lined with heavy plastic bags, large screw-top jars or airtight plastic containers or canisters you have on hand.

Premeasured Storage keeps just the amount you'll use in a specific recipe, so you won't have to measure it later. This is a good way to store SNACK CAKE MIX, MUFFIN MIX and the meat and seasoning mixes. You can use plastic containers such as margarine tubs, drink mix cans or shortening cans with lids. Or try potato chip canisters, glass jars or heavy-duty foil packets. Your storage equipment can be as creative as your imagination.

Labeling

Before you place a mix on the shelf or in the freezer, make sure it's properly labeled! Resist the urge to store a mix, then label it later, because later the mixes may all look alike! On each container, write the name of the mix and the date by which it should be used. In most instances the mixes can be stored longer than the specified time, but at the risk of loss in flavor, texture and nutrients. You may also want to write down the amount of mix in each container, particularly if you have divided the mix into premeasured amounts. In this case, you may want to record the page number of the mix recipe, too.

Master Mixes

Here they are—the road maps to all the recipes in this book. A casual glance will show you the wide variety of Master Mixes and the even wider variety of uses. QUICK MIX, for example, makes nearly 20 recipes! These mixes are your beginning to hundreds of breads, main dishes, appetizers, cookies and many types of desserts.

Basically, Master Mixes come in 3 types:

The Dry Mixes contain only dry ingredients and keep 6 to 8 months. Shake the mixes before you use them, as some ingredients may have settled during storage. Dry mixes include HOT ROLL MIX, SNACK CAKE MIX and MUFFIN MIX.

The Semi-Dry Mixes contain vegetable shortening, butter or margarine. These generally stay fresh for 10 to 12 weeks. Try WHEAT MIX, ALL-PURPOSE CAKE MIX and WHITE SAUCE MIX.

Freezer-Refrigerator Mixes are moist and require cold storage in appropriate containers. These keep well about 3 months. Keep a supply of ITALIAN-STYLE MEAT MIX, MEXICAN MEAT MIX and FREEZER PIE CRUST MIX for tasty, quick meals.

Be certain you familiarize yourself with the different kinds of Master Mixes and the many potential uses for each. You may find yourself creating new recipes with them! We recommend you start with QUICK MIX because of its versatility. Make up at least one main dish mix, such as CHICKEN MIX or ALL-PURPOSE GROUND BEEF MIX. Choose other mixes according to your particular tastes. How about MUFFIN MIX, BROWNIE MIX or BUTTERMILK PAN-CAKE AND WAFFLE MIX? Never let your shelves be without an ample supply of mixes.

Take time this weekend to make up a collection of mixes and discover your favorites. For a grand start, use BASIC COOKIE MIX to make many types of cookies at one time. Your family and friends will let you know how glad they are about your *Complete Make-a-Mix Cookbook*.

Quick Mix

The most versatile of all mixes!

8-1/2 cups all-purpose flour
4 tablespoons baking powder
1 tablespoon salt
2 teaspoons cream of tartar
1 teaspoon baking soda
1-1/2 cups instant nonfat dry
    milk or dry buttermilk
    powder
2-1/4 cups vegetable shortening

In a large bowl, sift together all dry ingredients. Blend well. With pastry blender or heavy-duty mixer, cut in shortening until mixture resembles cornmeal in texture. Put in a large airtight container. Label with date and contents. Store in a cool, dry place. Use within 10 to 12 weeks. Makes about 13 cups of QUICK MIX.

Variation
Use 4-1/4 cups all-purpose flour and 4-1/4 cups whole-wheat flour instead of 8-1/2 cups all-purpose flour. Increase baking powder to 5 tablespoons.

QUICK MIX makes:
Super-Duper Doughnuts, page 128
Sunshine Coffeecake, page 115
Madeline's Muffins, page 130
Nevada's Pancakes, page 121
Indian Fry Bread, page 129
Golden Cornbread, page 131
Crispy Breadsticks, page 131
Karine's Drop Biscuits, page 132
Never-Fail Rolled Biscuits, page 133
Curried Shrimp Rounds, page 51
Self-Crust Cheese Tart, page 77
Tuna-Cheese Swirls, page 88
Molasses Cookies, page 172
Carmel-Nut Pudding Cake, page 172
Hot Fudge Pudding Cake, page 173
Pineapple Upside-Down Cake, page 152
Impossible Pie, page 78
Turnover Fried Pies, page 151
Sunday Shortcake, page 173

Quick Mix makes, clockwise from top: Madeline's Muffins, page 130, Curried Shrimp Rounds, page 51, Caramel-Nut Pudding Cake, page 172, Turnover Fried Pies, page 151, Tuna-Cheese Swirls, page 88

Hot Roll Mix

Fix this ahead and you're ready to roll!

20 cups all-purpose flour
1-1/4 cups sugar
4 teaspoons salt
1 cup instant nonfat dry milk

Combine all ingredients in a large bowl. Stir together to distribute evenly. Put in a large airtight container. Label with date and contents. Store in a cool, dry place. Use within 6 to 8 months. Makes about 22 cups of HOT ROLL MIX.

Variation
Use 9 cups whole-wheat flour and 8 cups all-purpose flour instead of 20 cups all-purpose flour. Decrease sugar to 1 cup.

HOT ROLL MIX makes:

 *Muffin Mix*

Make many tempting muffins from one mix!

8 cups all-purpose flour
3 cups sugar
3 tablespoons baking powder
2 teaspoons salt
2 teaspoons ground cinnamon
2 teaspoons ground nutmeg

In a large bowl, combine flour, sugar, baking powder, salt, cinnamon and nutmeg. Mix well. Put in a large airtight container. Label with date and contents. Store in a cool, dry place. Use within 6 to 8 months. Makes about 11 cups of MUFFIN MIX.

MUFFIN MIX makes:

Melt-in-Your-Mouth Muffins, page 143
Molasses Bran Muffins, page 145
Apple Muffins, page 146
Cornmeal Muffins, page 145
Cranberry Cakes with Butter Sauce, page 154

 *Buttermilk Pancake and Waffle Mix*

Buttermilk powder is available in most supermarkets.

2 cups dry buttermilk powder
8 cups all-purpose flour
1/2 cup sugar
8 teaspoons baking powder
4 teaspoons baking soda
2 teaspoons salt

In a large bowl, combine all ingredients. Stir with a wire whisk until evenly distributed. Pour into a 12-cup container with a tight-fitting lid. Seal container. Label with date and contents. Store in a cool, dry place. Use within 6 months. Makes about 10-1/2 cups BUTTERMILK PANCAKE AND WAFFLE MIX.

BUTTERMILK PANCAKE AND WAFFLE MIX makes:

Aebleskivers, page 117
Buttermilk Pancakes, page 122
Buttermilk Waffles, page 118
Monte Cristo Sandwich, page 78
Puff Oven Pancake, page 118

Wheat Mix

Full of vitamins for delicious, mouth-watering meals.

6 cups whole-wheat flour
3 cups all-purpose flour
1-1/2 cups instant nonfat dry milk
1 tablespoon salt
1 cup sugar
1/2 cup wheat germ
1/4 cup baking powder
2 cups vegetable shorteninig

In a large bowl, combine whole-wheat flour, all-purpose flour, dry milk, salt, sugar, wheat germ and baking powder. Mix well. With a pastry blender or heavy-duty mixer, cut in shortening until mixture resembles cornmeal in texture. Put in a large airtight container. Label with date and contents. Store in a cool, dry place. Use within 10 to 12 weeks. Makes about 14 cups of WHEAT MIX.

WHEAT MIX makes:

Quick Wheat Breakfast Cake, page 119
Quick Wheat Muffins, page 146
Favorite Wheat Pancakes, page 119
Wheat Waffles, page 119
Coffeetime Quick Bread, page 120

Snack Cake Mix

One package SNACK CAKE MIX will make any of the cakes listed below.

8-3/4 cups all-purpose flour
2 tablespoons baking soda
1 tablespoon salt
5-1/4 cups granulated sugar

In a large bowl, combine all ingredients. Stir with a wire whisk until blended. Divide mixture evenly into six 2-1/2 cup containers with tight-fitting lids, about 2-1/4 cups each. Seal containers. Label with date and contents. Store in a cool dry place. Use within 10 to 12 weeks. Makes 6 packages or about 13-1/2 cups SNACK CAKE MIX.

SNACK CAKE MIX makes:

Applesauce Snack Cake, page 154
Banana-Walnut Snack Cake, page 155
Carrot Snack Cake, page 155
Date-Chocolate Chip Snack Cake, page 156
Double Chocolate Snack Cake, page 156
Gingerbread Snack Cake, page 157
Oatmeal Spice Cake, page 158

Sweet Quick Bread Mix

Brown sugar is always packed into the cup to insure a full measure.

6 cups all-purpose flour
1 tablespoon baking powder
1 tablespoon baking soda
1-1/2 teaspoons salt
1-1/2 cups granulated sugar
1-1/2 cups brown sugar, firmly
    packed
1-1/2 cups vegetable shortening

In a large bowl, stir flour, baking powder, baking soda, salt, granulated sugar and brown sugar with a large wire whisk until blended. Use a pastry blender or a heavy-duty mixer to blend in shortening until mixture resembles cornmeal in texture. Spoon into a 12-cup container with a tight-fitting lid. Seal container. Label with date and contents. Store in a cool, dry place. Use within 10 to 12 weeks. Makes about 11 cups SWEET QUICK BREAD MIX.

SWEET QUICK BREAD MIX makes:

Banana-Nut Bread, page 146
Carrot-Orange Loaf, page 147
Cranberry Bread, page 147
Date-Nut Bread, page 148
Pumpkin Bread, page 148
Spicy Applesauce Bread, page 149
Zucchini Bread, page 149

All-Purpose Cake Mix

Use this mix as you would a packaged cake mix.

10 cups all-purpose flour
6-1/4 cups sugar
1 cup cornstarch
5 tablespoons baking powder
1 tablespoon salt
2-1/2 cups vegetable shortening

In a large sifter, combine flour, sugar, cornstarch, baking powder and salt. Sift, in batches, into a large bowl. Use a pastry blender or a heavy-duty mixer to blend in shortening until mixture resembles cornmeal in texture. Spoon into a 20-cup container with a tight-fitting lid. Seal container. Label with date and contents. Store in a cool, dry place. Use within 10 to 12 weeks. Makes about 17 cups ALL-PURPOSE CAKE MIX.

ALL-PURPOSE CAKE MIX makes:

Chocolate Cake, page 157
Lemon Pound Cake, page 159
Yellow Cake, page 160
White Cake, page 160
Mom's Spumoni Cake, page 162

Vanilla Pudding and Pie Filling Mix

Vanilla is added when the mix is made into desserts.

2-1/3 cups granulated sugar
1-3/4 cups cornstarch
3/4 teaspoon salt

In a large bowl, combine all ingredients. Stir with a wire whisk until blended. Pour into a 4-cup container with a tight-fitting lid. Seal container. Label with date and contents. Store in a cool, dry place. Use within 4 months. Makes about 4 cups VANILLA PUDDING AND PIE FILLING MIX.

VANILLA PUDDING AND PIE FILLING MIX makes:
Boston Cream Pie, page 174
Creamy Vanilla Pudding, page 175
Layered Chocolate and Vanilla Dessert, page 175
Layered Vanilla Cream, page 176
Sour Cream and Raisin Pie, page 160
Vanilla Cream Pie, page 161

Chocolate Pudding and Pie Filling Mix

After you've used a wire whisk, you'll wonder how you ever got along without one.

1-1/2 cups plus 2 tablespoons
    unsweetened cocoa powder,
    sifted
3-1/4 cups granulated sugar
1-1/3 cups cornstarch
1/2 teaspoon salt

In a large bowl, combine all ingredients. Stir with a wire whisk until evenly distributed. Pour into a 6-cup container with a tight-fitting lid. Seal container. Label with date and contents. Store in a cool dry place. Use within 3 to 4 months. Makes about 6 cups CHOCOLATE PUDDING AND PIE FILLING MIX.

CHOCOLATE PUDDING and PIE FILLING MIX makes:
Chocolate Cream Pie, page 164
Chocolate-Filled Pirouette Cookies, page 177
Creamy Chocolate Pudding, page 175
Layered Chocolate and Vanilla Dessert, page 175

Lemon Pie Filling Mix

Tart and refreshing for a sauce or filling.

2-1/2 cups presweetened
    powdered lemonade mix
1 cup plus 2 tablespoons
    cornstarch
1-1/4 cups sugar, more for
    sweeter flavor
1 teaspoon salt

In a medium bowl, combine lemonade mix, cornstarch, sugar and salt. Mix well. Put in a 1-quart airtight container. Label with date and contents. Store in a cool, dry place. Use within 6 to 8 months. Makes about 4-1/4 cups LEMON PIE FILLING MIX.

LEMON PIE FILLING MIX makes:

Hot Lemon Sauce, page 176
Luscious Lemon Pie, page 164

Herbed Stuffing Mix

Keep this handy on the shelf for meat stuffing or tossed salad croutons!

30 slices firm-textured bread,
    cut in 1/2-inch cubes
2/3 cup cooking oil
3 tablespoons instant minced
    onion
3 tablespoons parsley flakes
2 teaspoons garlic salt
3/4 teaspoon ground sage
1/2 teaspoon seasoned pepper

Preheat oven to 300F (150C). Put bread cubes in two 13" x 9" baking pans. Toast bread cubes in oven for 45 minutes, stirring occasionally. Remove from oven and cool slightly. Stir in oil, onion, parsley flakes, garlic salt, sage and seasoned pepper. Lightly toss bread cubes with seasonings to coat cubes. Put in a large airtight container. Label with date and contents. Store in a cool, dry place. Use within 3 to 4 months. Makes about 12 cups HERBED STUFFING MIX.

HERBED STUFFING MIX makes:

Chicken Oahu, page 77
Supper Stuffing, page 70
Chicken Strata, page 82
Zucchini Casserole, page 74
Scallop Casserole, page 82
Sausage Cheese Breakfast Strata, page 120

Onion Seasoning Mix

Use this mix whenever your recipe calls for dry onion soup mix.

4 teaspoons instant beef bouillon
   granules
8 teaspoons dried minced onion
1 teaspoon onion powder
1/4 teaspoon Bon Appetit
   Seasoning

Cut a 6-inch square of heavy-duty foil. Place all ingredients in center of foil. Fold foil to make an airtight package. Label with date and contents. Store in a cool dry place. Use within 6 months. Makes 1 package ONION SEASONING MIX.

ONION SEASONING MIX makes:

Apricot Chicken, page 85
Company Beef Brisket, page 85
Cowboy Beans, page 70
French Onion Soup Gratiné, page 58
Meat and Potato Pie, page 112
No-Fuss Swiss Steak Cubes, page 83
Onion Pot Roast, page 83

Brownie Mix

For a quick after-school treat, keep this handy!

6 cups all-purpose flour
4 teaspoons baking powder
4 teaspoons salt
8 cups sugar
1 (8-oz.) can unsweetened cocoa
　　powder
2 cups vegetable shortening

In a large bowl, sift together flour, baking powder and salt. Add sugar and cocoa. Blend well. With a pastry blender or heavy-duty mixer, cut in shortening until mixture resembles cornmeal in texture. Put in a large airtight container. Label with date and contents. Store in a cool, dry place. Use within 10 to 12 weeks. Makes about 17 cups of BROWNIE MIX.

BROWNIE MIX makes:

Chewy Chocolate Cookies, page 177
Our Best Brownies, page 178
Texas Sheet Cake, page 165
Fudge Sauce, page 67
Brownie Alaska, page 179
Mississippi Mud, page 180

Basic Cookie Mix

With this versatile mix you gain time, money and variety.

8 cups all-purpose flour
2-1/2 cups granulated sugar
2 cups brown sugar, firmly
　　packed
4 teaspoons salt
1-1/2 teaspoons baking soda
3 cups vegetable shortening

In a large bowl, combine flour, granulated sugar, brown sugar, salt and baking soda until well-blended. With a pastry blender or heavy-duty mixer, cut in shortening until mixture resembles cornmeal in texture. Put in a large airtight container. Label with date and contents. Store in a cool, dry place. Use within 10 to 12 weeks. Makes about 16 cups of BASIC COOKIE MIX.

BASIC COOKIE MIX makes:

Tropic Macaroons, page 180
Snickerdoodles, page 179
Chocolate Chip Cookies, page 181
Banana-Coconut Delights, page 181
Peanut Butter Cookies, page 181

Cookie Crumb Crust Mix

In great taste whenever your recipes call for a crumb crust.

6 cups all-purpose flour
1-1/2 cups chopped nuts
1-1/2 cups brown sugar, firmly
    packed
1 lb. butter or margarine,
    softened

Preheat oven to 375F (190C). In a large bowl, combine flour, nuts and brown sugar. Blend well. With a pastry blender or heavy-duty mixer, cut in butter or margarine until mixture resembles cornmeal in texture. Press mixture firmly into 2 unbuttered, shallow baking pans. Bake about 15 minutes. Cool. Crumble and put in a large airtight container. Label with date and contents. Store in a cool, dry place. Use within 4 to 6 weeks. Makes about 10-1/2 cups COOKIE CRUMB CRUST MIX.

Cookie Crumb Crust

To make a single crust: Press about 2 cups crumb mix into a baking pan or 9-inch pie plate and bake according to directions for filling.

COOKIE CRUMB CRUST MIX makes:

Banana Split Cake, page 182
Lemonade Ice Cream Dessert, page 184
Blueberry Dessert, page 182

Graham Cracker Crust Mix

With this mix, you'll crumb enough crackers for six crusts and have only one clean-up.

1 (2-1b.) box graham crackers
1 cup granulated sugar
2 teaspoons ground cinnamon

Process 6 or 7 crackers in blender or food processor fitted with the metal blade to make fine crumbs. Pour crumbs into a large bowl. Repeat with remaining crackers. Or use a rolling pin to crush crackers between 2 sheets of waxed paper or in a plastic bag. Stir in sugar and cinnamon. Pour into a 10-cup container with a tight-fitting lid. Seal container. Label with date and contents. Store in a cool dry place. Use within 6 months. Makes about 9 cups GRAHAM CRACKER CRUST MIX.

Graham Cracker Pie and Dessert Crust

To make crust for 9-inch pie plate, springform pan or baking dish: Combine 1-1/2 cups GRAHAM CRACKER CRUST MIX, page 21, with 1/3 cup melted butter or margarine. If baking crust, preheat oven to 375F (190C). Press mixture firmly over bottom and up side of pie plate or springform pan; or press firmly into bottom of 8- or 9-inch baking dish. Refrigerate 45 minutes before filling, or bake 6 to 8 minutes in preheated oven; cool completely before adding filling. Fill as desired. Makes one 8- or 9-inch crust.

GRAHAM CRACKER CRUST MIX makes:

Chocolate-Marshmallow Dessert, page 184
Chocolate-Peppermint Supreme, page 185
Lemon Light Dessert, page 184
Our Favorite Cheesecake, page 185

White Sauce Mix

White Sauce makes meats and vegetables into meals fit for a king.

2 cups instant nonfat dry milk,
   or 1-1/2 cups regular nonfat
   dry milk
1 cup all-purpose flour
2 teaspoons salt
1 cup butter or margarine

In a large bowl, combine dry milk, flour and salt. Mix well. With a pastry blender, cut in butter or margarine until mixture resembles fine crumbs. Put in a large airtight container. Label with date and contents. Store in refrigerator. Use within 2 months. Makes 1 quart of WHITE SAUCE MIX, enough for about 8 cups Basic White Sauce, page 58.

WHITE SAUCE MIX makes:
Basic White Sauce, page 58
Cream of Chicken Soup, page 61
Eastern Corn Chowder, page 61
Hearty New England Clam Chowder, page 59
Company Chicken Roll-Ups, page 86
Potatoes Au Gratin, page 70
Broccoli Cheese Soup in Bread Bowls, page 59

Oriental Stir-Fry Mix

Cut the bark-like skin off the gingerroot, then shred the root on a fine-hole grater.

6 tablespoons cornstarch
3/4 teaspoon garlic powder
2-1/4 teaspoons instant beef
   bouillon granules
3/4 teaspoon onion powder
6 tablespoons wine vinegar
6 tablespoons water
1-1/2 teaspoons freshly grated
   gingerroot
3/4 cup soy sauce
3/4 cup dark corn syrup
2-2/3 cups water

In a large bowl, combine cornstarch, garlic powder, bouillon granules and onion powder. Use a wire whisk to stir in vinegar, 6 tablespoons water and gingerroot until cornstarch is dissolved. Stir in soy sauce, corn syrup and 2-2/3 cups water. Pour into a 5-cup container with a tight-fitting lid. Attach lid. Label container with date and contents. Store in refrigerator. Use within 4 weeks. Stir well before using. Makes about 5 cups ORIENTAL STIR-FRY MIX.

ORIENTAL STIR-FRY MIX makes:
Teriyaki Beef and Vegetables, page 88
Shrimp and Vegetable Stir-Fry, page 87
Stir-Fry Cashew Chicken, page 87

Freezer Cheese Sauce Mix

Try topping baked potatoes with this mix, then sprinkle with crumbled cooked bacon.

3/4 cup all-purpose flour
1-1/2 teaspoons salt
1/4 teaspoon ground nutmeg
3/4 cup butter or margarine
4 cups milk
2 cups condensed chicken broth
1 cup half-and-half
4 egg yolks, beaten
3 cups shredded Cheddar cheese
  (12 oz.)

In a small bowl, combine flour, salt and nutmeg; set aside. In a heavy large saucepan, melt butter or margarine over medium heat. Gradually stir in flour mixture, milk and chicken broth until smooth. Cook and stir over medium-high heat until smooth and slightly thickened, about 2 minutes. Remove from heat. In a medium bowl, stir half-and-half into egg yolks. Blend in about half of the hot sauce. Stir egg mixture into remaining sauce. Cook and stir over medium heat about 2 minutes; do not boil. Remove from heat. Stir in cheese until melted. Cool to room temperature. Refrigerate sauce until completely cooled. Pour about 1-1/3 cups sauce into each of 6 freezer containers with tight-fitting lids. Leave 1-inch air space at top of each container. Attach lids. Label containers with date and contents. Store in freezer. Use within 6 months. Makes 6 packages or about 8 cups FREEZER CHEESE SAUCE MIX.

FREEZER CHEESE SAUCE MIX makes:

Cauliflower Fritters in Cheese Sauce, page 71
Cheese Fondue, page 52
English Poached Eggs and Ham, page 121
Old-Fashioned Vegetable Platter, page 72
Puffy Omelet, page 122

Meat Sauce Mix

It's a lifesaver on those extra-busy days.

1/4 cup vegetable shortening
4 medium onions, sliced
3 garlic cloves, finely chopped,
    or 3/8 teaspoon instant
    minced garlic
2 cups finely chopped celery
2 to 3 chopped carrots, if desired
5 lbs. lean ground beef
5 teaspoons salt
1/2 teaspoon pepper
3 tablespoons Worcestershire
    sauce
1 (28-oz.) bottle ketchup
6 drops hot pepper sauce

Melt shortening in a large skillet over medium heat. Add onions, garlic, celery and carrots, if desired. Sauté until onions are golden. Add ground beef. Stir and cook until meat is browned. Add salt, pepper, Worcestershire sauce, ketchup and hot pepper sauce. Cover and simmer 20 minutes. Drain excess fat. Cool. Put into five 2-cup freezer containers, leaving 1/2-inch space at top. Cut through mixture with a knife several times to remove air spaces. Seal and label containers with date and contents. Freeze. Use within 3 months. Makes about 5 pints of MEAT SAUCE MIX.

MEAT SAUCE MIX makes:

Speedy Pizza, page 53
Rancher's Sloppy Joes, page 86
Stuffed Hard Rolls, page 90
Stuffed Green Peppers, page 90
Hamburger Trio Skillet, page 90
Hamburger-Noodle Skillet, page 91
Layered Casserole Complete, page 92
Chili Con Carne, page 91

1. Sauté the onions, garlic and celery over medium heat until the onions are golden. Add ground beef.

2. Cook until the meat is browned, then add spices, Worcestershire sauce, ketchup and hot pepper sauce.

Meatball Mix

Meatballs are always ready—for appetizers, casseroles and main dishes.

4 lbs. lean ground beef
4 eggs, slightly beaten
2 cups dry bread crumbs
1/2 cup finely chopped onion
1 tablespoon salt
2 tablespoons cornstarch
1/4 teaspoon pepper
2 teaspoons Worcestershire sauce

Preheat oven to 400F (205C). Combine all ingredients in a large bowl. Blend well. Shape mixture into 1-inch balls. Place meatballs on ungreased baking sheets and bake 10 to 15 minutes, until browned. Remove immediately and drain on paper towels. When cooled, put about 30 meatballs each into five 1-quart freezer containers, leaving 1/2-inch space at top. Seal and label containers with date and contents. Freeze. Use within 3 months. Makes about 144 meatballs.

MEATBALL MIX makes:

Cocktail Meatballs, page 53
Sweet and Sour Meatballs, page 91
Meatball Stew, page 92

Italian Cooking Sauce Mix

Superb, savory and simple.

2 (14-1/2-oz.) cans stewed
   tomatoes, pureed
4 (8-oz.) cans tomato sauce
2 cups water
2 (6-oz.) cans tomato paste
2 tablespoons instant minced
   onion
2 tablespoons parsley flakes
3 teaspoons salt
2 tablespoons cornstarch
4 teaspoons green pepper flakes
1 teaspoon instant minced garlic
3 teaspoons sugar
1-1/2 teaspoons Italian
   seasoning

Combine all ingredients in a large kettle or Dutch oven. Simmer 15 minutes over medium-low heat. Cool. Put into six 2 cup freezer containers, leaving 1/2-inch space at top. Seal and label containers. Freeze. Use within 6 months. Makes about 6 pints of ITALIAN COOKING SAUCE MIX.

ITALIAN COOKING SAUCE MIX makes:

Stuffed Manicotti Shells, page 98
Veal Parmigiana, page 99
Chicken Cacciatore, page 98
Last-Minute Lasagna, page 99

Italian-Style Meat Mix

Butchers often have pork bones they will give away.

3 lbs. sweet Italian sausage, cut
 in 2-inch lengths
2 (28-oz.) cans tomato puree
1 (28-oz.) can peeled tomatoes,
 slightly mashed
1-1/2 teaspoons dried sweet basil
 leaves, crushed
1-1/4 teaspoons dried parsley
 leaves, crushed
1 teaspoon granulated sugar
1/4 teaspoon pepper
1/2 teaspoon garlic powder
5 teaspoons grated Romano
 cheese
6 cups water
1-1/2 lbs. pork bones
Meatballs, see below

Meatballs:
1-1/2 lbs. lean ground beef
1/2 teaspoon dried sweet basil
 leaves, crushed
1/4 teaspoon onion powder
1/2 teaspoon dried parsley
 leaves, crushed
1/2 teaspoon salt
1/4 teaspoon pepper
1/2 cup soft bread crumbs
1 egg, beaten

In a large skillet or Dutch oven, brown Italian sausage over medium-high heat, stirring occasionally. Simmer over low heat 20 to 25 minutes longer until meat is no longer pink. Drain, reserving 2 tablespoons drippings in skillet. Stir in tomato puree, tomatoes, basil, parsley, sugar, pepper, garlic powder, Romano cheese, water and pork bones. Cover; simmer 30 minutes over medium heat. Prepare meatballs. Spoon meatballs into tomato mixture. Bring to a boil over medium-high heat. Cover; simmer over low heat 5 to 6 hours until thickened. Remove pork bones. Cool meatball mixture in skillet on a rack. Spoon into freezer containers in amounts shown in recipes listed below. Leave 1/2 inch air space at top of each container. Attach lids. Label containers with date, contents and quantity. Store in freezer. Use within 6 months. Makes about 16 cups ITALIAN-STYLE MEAT MIX.

Meatballs

Preheat oven to 400F (205C). Combine all ingredients in a medium bowl. Shape into 1-inch balls. Place meatballs on an ungreased baking sheet with raised sides. Bake 10 to 15 minutes in preheated oven until browned. Remove meatballs from baking sheet. Discard drippings.

ITALIAN-STYLE MEAT MIX makes:
Cathy's Meatball Sandwiches, page 97
Eggplant Parmesan, page 97
Green Peppers Italian-Style, page 74
Spaghetti Royale, page 98
Italian-Style Zucchini, page 72
Last-Minute Lasagna, page 99

Mexican Meat Mix

Guaranteed to please your guests.

5 lbs. beef roast or combination
    of beef and pork roasts
3 tablespoons vegetable
    shortening
3 onions, chopped
1 (4-oz.) can chopped green
    chilies
2 (7-oz.) cans green chili salsa
1/4 teaspoon garlic powder
4 tablespoons all-purpose flour
4 teaspoons salt
1 teaspoon ground cumin
Juices from beef roasts

Preheat oven to 275F (135C). Place roasts in large roasting pan or Dutch Oven. Do not add salt or water. Cover with a tight lid and roast about 8-10 hours, until well done. Or cook roasts with 1 cup water in pressure cooker 35 to 40 minutes. Drain meat, reserving juices. Cool meat, then remove bones. Shred meat, and set aside. Melt shortening in a large skillet. Add onions and green chilies. Sauté 1 minute. Add green chili salsa, garlic powder, flour, salt and cumin. Cook 1 minute over medium-low heat. Stir in reserved meat juices and shredded meat. Cook 5 minutes until thick. Cool. Put about 3 cups mix each into three 1-quart freezer containers, leaving 1/2-inch space at top. Seal and label containers with date and contents. Freeze. Use within 6 months. Makes about 9 cups of MEXICAN MEAT MIX.

MEXICAN MEAT MIX makes:

Green Chili Burros, page 92
Chalupa, page 94
Chimichangas, page 94
Sour Cream Enchiladas, page 96
Tacos Supreme, page 96
Mini-Chimis, page 54

Cubed Pork Mix

To get the most from your meat, have your butcher cube a center cut of pork shoulder.

1/4 cup butter or margarine
5 lbs. boneless lean pork, cubed
3 medium onions, sliced
3/4 cup all-purpose flour
About 3-1/2 cups water
4 teaspoons instant chicken
  bouillon granules or 4
  chicken bouillon cubes
2-1/2 teaspoons salt
1/2 teaspoon pepper

In a large skillet, melt butter or margarine over medium-high heat. Add pork cubes. Cook until lightly browned, stirring occasionally. Drain as drippings collect; reserve drippings. Add onions to browned pork cubes. Cook 10 to 15 minutes until onions are soft and golden, stirring occasionally. Sprinkle flour over pork mixture. Stir gently until flour is absorbed, about 1 minute. Add water to drippings to make 4 cups liquid. Stir liquid mixture, bouillon granules or bouillon cubes, salt and pepper into pork mixture. Bring mixture to a boil, stirring occasionally to loosen drippings in pan. Cover; cook over low heat about 2 hours longer until pork is tender. Remove from heat. Cool on a rack. Ladle mixture into five 2-cup freezer containers with tight-fitting lids, leaving 1/2-inch space at top of each. Attach lids. Label containers with date and contents. Store in freezer. Use within 6 months. Makes 5 packages or about 10 cups CUBED PORK MIX.

CUBED PORK MIX makes:

Hurry-Up Curry, page 102
Pork Chow Mein, page 100
Pork Noodles, page 62
Quick Chow Mein, page 104
Sweet and Sour Pork, page 100
Won Tons, page 55

1. Add onions to browned meat. Cook until onions are tender. Simmer 2 hours with remaining ingredients.

2. Spoon into five 2-cup freezer containers, leaving a 1/2-inch space at top. Label and store in freezer.

All-Purpose Ground Beef Mix

This very basic mix can be used in most casseroles that call for a meat mixture.

5 lbs. lean ground beef
1 tablespoon salt
2 cups chopped celery
2 cups chopped onions
1 cup diced green pepper

In a large pot or Dutch oven, brown ground beef over medium-high heat, stirring to break up meat. Drain; discard drippings. Stir in salt, celery, onions and green pepper. Cover; simmer over low heat until vegetables are crisp-tender, about 10 minutes. Remove from heat; cool on a rack. Ladle into six 2-cup freezer containers with tight-fitting lids, leaving 1/2-inch air space at top of each. Cut through mixture in each container with a knife several times to remove air pockets. Attach lids. Label containers with date and contents. Store in freezer. Use within 3 months. Makes 6 packages or about 12 cups ALL-PURPOSE GROUND BEEF MIX.

ALL-PURPOSE GROUND BEEF MIX makes:

Best-Ever Minestrone Soup, page 62
Company Casserole, page 101
Dinner-in-a-Pumpkin, page 101
Hearty Beef Chowder, page 64
Saturday Stroganoff, page 102
Enchilada Casserole, page 102
Hurry-Up Curry, page 102
Mexican Delight, page 103
Oriental-Style Hamburger Skillet, page 103
Quick Chow Mein, page 104
Slumgullion, page 105
Spaghetti Casserole, page 105
Taco Salad, page 64
Quick Taco Dip, page 52

# Chicken Mix

12 to 14 whole chicken breasts may be substituted for fryers.

*11 lbs. chicken (4 medium
  fryers), cut up*
4 qts. cold water
3 tablespoons parsley flakes
4 carrots, peeled and chopped
4 teaspoons salt
1/2 teaspoon pepper
2 teaspoon basil leaves

Combine all ingredients in a large kettle or Dutch oven. Cover and cook over high heat until water boils. Simmer until meat is tender, about 1-1/2 hours. Remove from heat. Strain broth and refrigerate until fat can be skimmed. Cool chicken, then remove and discard bones and skin. Put chicken into six 1-pint freezer containers, leaving 1/2-inch space at top. Pour skimmed chicken broth into six more 1-pint containers, with 1/2-inch space at top. Seal and label containers with date and contents. Freeze. Use within 3 months. Makes about 6 pints of CHICKEN MIX and about 6 pints of chicken broth.

CHICKEN MIX makes:

Five-Way Beef Mix

By using a food processor to dice or chop the vegetables, you'll cut the work in half.

5 lbs. lean ground beef or lean
    beef cubes
4 onions, chopped, or 1 cup
    dried chopped onions
3 tablespoons vegetable oil, if
    using beef cubes
About 1 cup water, if using beef
    cubes
8 cups diced peeled potatoes
6 cups diced peeled carrots
1/3 cup cornstarch
1/2 cup cold water
1 (24-oz.) pkg. frozen peas,
    partially thawed
4 teaspoons seasoning salt
2 teaspoons ground sage
1 teaspoon salt
1 teaspoon pepper

Brown ground beef and onions in a large skillet over medium heat; set aside. Or heat oil in skillet; add beef cubes and onions. Cook until cubes are browned. Add about 1 cup water to browned beef cubes. Cover and simmer over low heat until tender, about 1 hour, adding more water if needed. Place potatoes and carrots in a 5-quart Dutch oven. Add water to barely cover. Bring to a boil. Simmer vegetables over medium heat until crisp-tender, about 15 minutes. Stir cornstarch into 1/2 cup cold water. Stir into vegetable mixture until liquid is slightly thickened. Stir in remaining ingredients. Stir in browned beef mixture. Cool on a rack. Ladle mix into four 6-cup freezer containers with tight-fitting lids, leaving 1/2-inch air space. Stir to remove air pockets. Attach lids. Label with date and contents. Store in freezer. Use within 2 months. Makes 4 packages or about 24 cups FIVE-WAY BEEF MIX.

FIVE-WAY BEEF MIX makes:

Bread Basket Stew, page 80
Deep-Dish Pot Pie, page 111
Grandma's Hamburger Soup, page 66
Swiss Hamburger Soup, page 67
Vegetable and Cheese Casserole, page 112

 *Freezer Pie Crust Mix*

If you usually use a 10-inch pie plate, divide the dough into 6 rolls instead of 7 rolls.

6 cups all-purpose flour
2 teaspoons salt
1(1-lb.) can vegetable shortening
  (2-1/3 cups)
1-1/4 to 1-1/2 cups cold water

Cut seven 12-inch squares of plastic wrap and heavy-duty foil; set aside. In a large bowl, combine flour and salt. With pastry blender or heavy-duty mixer, cut in shortening until mixture resembles cornmeal in texture. Add 1-1/4 cups water all at once. Mix lightly with a fork until water is absorbed and mixture forms a ball. If necessary add additional water. Divide dough into 7 equal portions. Shape each portion into a ball. Flatten each ball slightly. Wrap each flattened ball in 1 piece of plastic wrap. Place 1 wrapped ball on each piece of foil. Fold foil tightly against ball, making an airtight seal. Label each package with date and contents. Store in freezer. Use within 10 months. Makes 7 packages of FREEZER PIE CRUST MIX, enough for seven 8- or 9-inch single crust pies.

Freezer Pie Crust

To make single pie crust: Completely thaw 1 package FREEZER PIE CRUST MIX. If baking empty crust, preheat oven to 450F (230C). On a lightly floured pastry cloth or between two 12-inch pieces of lightly floured plastic wrap, roll out dough to an 11-inch circle. Dough will be quite thin. Remove plastic wrap, if used. Carefully fit rolled-out dough into an 8- or 9-inch pie plate without stretching dough. Trim and flute edge. Prick crust with the tines of a fork. Bake about 10 minutes in preheated oven until lightly browned. Or add filling and bake according to filling directions. To make double crust pie: Completely thaw 2 packages FREEZER PIE CRUST MIX. Prepare 1 ball of dough according to directions above; do not prick crust or flute edge. Turn filling into shell. Roll out top crust. Place over filling. Press edges together; flute pressed edges. Cut small slits in top crust to let steam escape. Bake according to directions for filling.

FREEZER PIE CRUST MIX makes:

Cherry-Almond Pie, page 166
Chocolate Cream Pie, page 164
Deep-Dish Pot Pie, page 111
Fresh Peach Pie, page 165
Meat and Potato Pie, page 112
All-American Apple Pie, page 166
Simplified Quiche, page 123
Luscious Lemon Pie, page 164
Sour Cream and Lemon Pie, page 169
Sour Cream and Raisin Pie, page 160
Spanish Cheese Pie, page 113
Turkey Dinner Pie, page 113
Vanilla Cream Pie, page 161

Cream Cheese Pastry Mix

Thaw the dough completely before you roll it out. It will take about four hours.

4 (3-oz.) pkgs. cream cheese,
   softened
1 lb. butter or margarine,
   softened
5 cups all-purpose flour

Cut eight 12-inch squares of plastic wrap and heavy-duty foil; set aside. In a large bowl, beat cream cheese and butter or margarine until blended. Add flour all at once. Knead in flour until evenly distributed. Shape into a large ball. Divide into 8 smaller balls. Slightly flatten each ball. Wrap each flattened ball in a piece of plastic wrap. Place 1 wrapped ball on each piece of foil. Fold foil tightly against dough, making an airtight seal. Label each package with date and contents. Store in freezer. Use within 6 months. Makes 8 packages CREAM CHEESE PASTRY MIX, enough for 8 single-crust pies, 4 double-crust pies or 80 tart shells.

Cream Cheese Pastry

To make single-crust pie, completely thaw 1 package CREAM CHEESE PASTRY MIX. If baking empty crust, pre-heat oven to 450F (230C). On a lightly floured pastry cloth or between 2 lightly floured pieces of plastic wrap, roll out dough to an 11-inch circle. Carefully fit rolled-out dough into an 8- or 9-inch pie plate without stretching dough. Trim and flute edge. Prick crust with the tines of a fork. Bake about 10 minutes in preheated oven until lightly browned. Or add filling and bake according to filling directions. To make double-crust pie: Completely thaw 2 packages CREAM CHEESE PASTRY MIX. Prepare 1 ball of dough according to directions above; do not prick crust or flute edge. Turn filling into shell. Roll out top crust. Place over filling. Press edges together; flute pressed edges. Cut small slits in top crust to let steam escape. Bake according to directions for filling. To make tart shells, completely thaw 2 packages CREAM CHEESE PASTRY MIX. Divide each package into 10 pieces. Shape each piece into a ball. Preheat oven to 400F (205C). Place each ball in a medium muffin cup. Use your thumbs to press dough over bottom and up side of each cup, keeping dough at an even thickness. Bake in preheated oven 10 to 12 minutes or until lightly browned. Cool and remove from cups. Fill with desired filling.

CREAM CHEESE PASTRY MIX makes:

Almond Kringle, page 123
Chess Tarts, page 168

Special Mixes

Special Mixes differ from Master Mixes in that they are designed primarily for one recipe while Master Mixes make several recipes. This is where you'll find the seasoning mixes, salad dressing mixes, beverages, dips and side dishes. The recipe made by each Special Mix follows the mix itself. Most of the Special Mixes are dry mixes which keep about 6 months.

You will note that Special Mixes resemble commercial seasoning mixes you find on your grocer's shelves. They can be used whenever you would use a similar packaged mix. The advantages of making your own Special Mixes rather than purchasing them are fresher flavor, lower cost and lack of additives.

With the exception of the beverage mixes, most Special Mixes should be stored in proportions for individual recipes for your convenience. Foil packets or small plastic bags are great for this purpose. The dry beverage mixes are most easily stored in large canisters. Remember that HOT CHOCOLATE MIX makes 34 cups of mix, enough for 100 cups of Hot Chocolate; FRUIT SLUSH MIX and MARIE'S FRUIT COCKTAIL MIX should be frozen according to recipe directions.

For added convenience, try storing the Salad Dressing Mixes in containers large enough for you to add the remaining ingredients. Then you can just shake them up at serving time! It makes *The Complete Make-a-Mix Cookbook* even easier.

When preparing Seasoning Mixes, remember to label them before storing. They are often difficult to distinguish from one another later.

We know you will enjoy having Special Mixes made ahead and ready on your shelves. Start making extra batches of your favorites. Our favorites include HOME-STYLE DRESSING MIX, MARIE'S FRUIT COCKTAIL MIX and CHEESE FILLED LASAGNA OR MANICOTTI ROLLS. When you serve the dip mixes at a party, be sure to have copies of the recipe close at hand. These dips guarantee "rave reviews."

Mixes make great gifts, too. A new bride will be grateful for such a creative gift. Package them in appropriate containers and include the recipes that go along with the mix.

Special Mix beverages, clockwise from top: Orange Float, page 43, Fruit Slush, page 44, Marie's Fruit Cocktail, page 43, Hot Chocolate, page 42, Russian Refresher, page 42.

Priscilla's Salad Dressing Mix

Make the dressing given below, then serve it over a spinach salad topped with crumbled bacon.

1/2 cup granulated sugar
1 teaspoon salt
1 teaspoon dry mustard
1 tablespoon poppy seeds
1 tablespoon dried minced onion

Combine all ingredients in a small bowl, stirring until evenly distributed. Pour into a 1/2-cup container with a tight-fitting lid or wrap airtight in heavy-duty foil. Seal container. Label with date and contents. Store in a cool dry place. Use within 3 months. Makes 1 package or about 1/3 cup PRISCILLA'S SALAD DRESSING MIX.

Priscilla's Salad Dressing

1-1/2 cups small-curd cottage
    cheese (12 oz.)
1 pkg. PRISCILLA'S SALAD
    DRESSING MIX, see above
1 cup vegetable oil
1/2 cup vinegar

Turn cottage cheese into a medium bowl; set aside. In a blender, combine PRISCILLA'S SALAD DRESSING MIX, oil and vinegar. Blend 5 to 8 seconds. Pour over cottage cheese. Fold oil mixture into cottage cheese until just blended. Cover; refrigerate 30 minutes before serving. Makes about 3 cups.

Home-Style Dressing Mix

Your own version of that famous dressing.

2 teaspoons instant minced
    onion
1/2 teaspoon salt
1/8 teaspoon garlic powder
1/2 teaspoon monosodium
    glutamate, if desired
1 tablespoon parsley flakes

Combine all ingredients in a small bowl until evenly distributed. Put mixture in foil packet or 1-pint glass jar. Label with date and contents. Store in a cool, dry place. Use within 6 months. Makes about 2 tablespoons HOME-STYLE DRESSING MIX, enough for 2 cups Home-Style Dressing.

Home-Style Dressing

1 recipe HOME-STYLE
    DRESSING MIX, see above
1 cup mayonnaise
1 cup buttermilk

Combine ingredients in a glass jar. Shake until well blended. Chill before serving. Makes about 2 cups Home-Style Dressing.

Variation
Substitute 1 cup sour cream for buttermilk and use as a dip for fresh vegetables.

Sloppy Joe Seasoning Mix

So easy and so good!

1 tablespoon instant minced
    onion
1 teaspoon green pepper flakes
1 teaspoon salt
1 teaspoon cornstarch
1/2 teaspoon instant minced
    garlic
1/4 teaspoon dry mustard
1/4 teaspoon celery seed
1/4 teaspoon chili powder

Combine all ingredients in a small bowl until evenly distributed. Spoon mixture onto a 6-inch square of aluminum foil and fold to make airtight. Label with date and contents. Store in a cool, dry place. Use within 6 months. Makes 1 package or about 3 tablespoons SLOPPY JOE SEASONING MIX.

Sloppy Joes

1 lb. lean ground beef
1 pkg. SLOPPY JOE
    SEASONING MIX, see above
1/2 cup water
1 (8-oz.) can tomato sauce
6 hamburger buns, toasted

Brown ground beef in a medium skillet over medium-high heat. Drain excess grease. Add SLOPPY JOE SEASONING MIX, water and tomato sauce. Bring to a boil. Reduce heat and simmer 10 minutes, stirring occasionally. Serve over toasted hamburger buns. Makes 6 servings.

Chili Seasoning Mix

You'd better double the recipe!

1 tablespoon all-purpose flour
2 tablespoons instant minced
    onion
1-1/2 teaspoons chili powder
1 teaspoon seasoned salt
1/2 teaspoon crushed dried red
    pepper
1/2 teaspoon instant minced
    garlic
1/2 teaspoon sugar
1/2 teaspoon ground cumin

Combine all ingredients in a small bowl until evenly distributed. Spoon mixture onto a 6-inch square of aluminum foil and fold to make airtight. Label with date and contents. Store in a cool dry place. Use within 6 months. Makes 1 package or about 1/4 cup CHILI SEASONING MIX.

Variation
For a special treat, sprinkle CHILI SEASONING MIX over hot popcorn.

Chili

1 lb. lean ground beef
2 (15-1/2-oz.) cans kidney beans
2 (16-oz.) cans tomatoes
1 pkg. CHILI SEASONING
    MIX, see above

Brown ground beef in a medium skillet over medium-high heat. Drain. Add kidney beans, tomatoes and CHILI SEASONING MIX. Reduce heat and simmer 10 minutes, stirring occasionally. Makes 4 to 6 servings.

Taco Seasoning Mix

Your tacos will be hot and spicy!

2 teaspoons instant minced
    onion
1 teaspoon salt
1 teaspoon chili powder
1/2 teaspoon cornstarch
1/2 teaspoon crushed dried red
    pepper
1/2 teaspoon instant minced
    garlic
1/4 teaspoon dried oregano
1/2 teaspoon ground cumin

Combine all ingredients in a small bowl until evenly distributed. Spoon mixture onto a 6-inch square of aluminum foil and fold to make airtight. Label with date and contents. Store in a cool, dry place. Use within 6 months. Makes 1 package or about 2 tablespoons TACO SEASONING MIX.

Taco Filling

1-1/2 lbs. lean ground beef
1/2 cup water
1 pkg. TACO SEASONING
    MIX, see above

Brown ground beef in a medium skillet over medium-high heat. Drain excess grease. Add water and TACO SEASONING MIX. Reduce heat and simmer 10 minutes, stirring occasionally. Makes filling for 8 to 10 tacos.

Spaghetti Seasoning Mix

It makes great lasagna and pizza sauce, too!

1 tablespoon instant minced
  onion
1 tablespoon parsley flakes
1 tablespoon cornstarch
2 teaspoons green pepper flakes
1-1/2 teaspoons salt
1/4 teaspoon instant minced
  garlic
1 teaspoon sugar
3/4 teaspoon Italian seasoning
  or combination of Italian
  herbs (oregano, basil,
  rosemary, thyme, sage,
  marjoram)

Combine all ingredients in a small bowl until evenly distributed. Spoon mixture onto a 6-inch square of aluminum foil and fold to make airtight. Label with date and contents. Store in a cool, dry place. Use within 6 months. Makes 1 package or about 1/3 cup SPAGHETTI SEASONING MIX.

Spaghetti Sauce

1 lb. lean ground beef
2 (8-oz.) cans tomato sauce
1 (6-oz.) can tomato paste
2-3/4 cups tomato juice or water
1 pkg. SPAGHETTI
  SEASONING MIX, see above

Brown ground beef in a medium skillet over medium-high heat. Drain excess grease. Add tomato sauce, tomato paste and tomato juice or water. Stir in SPAGHETTI SEASONING MIX. Reduce heat and simmer 30 minutes, stirring occasionally. Makes 4 to 6 servings.

Creamy Crudité Dip Mix

The ideal place to put fresh garden vegetables.

1 tablespoon dried chives
1/2 teaspoon dill weed
1 teaspoon garlic salt
1/2 teaspoon paprika

Combine all ingredients in a small bowl until evenly distributed. Spoon mixture onto a 6-inch square of aluminum foil and fold to make airtight. Label with date and contents. Store in a cool, dry place. Use within 6 months. Makes 1 package or about 2 tablespoons CREAMY CRUDITÉ DIP MIX.

Creamy Crudité Dip

1 tablespoon lemon juice
1 cup mayonnaise
1 cup dairy sour cream
1 pkg. CREAMY CRUDITÉ
  DIP MIX, see above

Combine all ingredients. Chill at least 1 hour before serving. Makes about 2 cups of Creamy Crudité Dip.

Crunchy Granola Mix

Serve with milk for breakfast or as a great afternoon snack by itself.

10 cups old-fashioned rolled
   oats
1 cup wheat germ
1/2 lb. shredded coconut
2 cups raw sunflower seeds
1 cup sesame seeds
3 cups chopped almonds,
   pecans, walnuts or
   combination
1-1/2 cups brown sugar, firmly
   packed
1-1/2 cups water
1-1/2 cups vegetable oil
1/2 cup honey
1/2 cup molasses
1-1/2 teaspoons salt
2 teaspoons ground cinnamon
3 teaspoons vanilla extract
Raisins or other dried fruits, if
   desired

Preheat oven to 300F (150C). In a large bowl combine oats, wheat germ, coconut, sunflower seeds, sesame seeds and nuts. Blend well. In a large saucepan, combine brown sugar, water, oil, honey, molasses, salt, cinnamon and vanilla. Heat until sugar is dissolved, but do not boil. Pour syrup over dry ingredients and stir until well-coated. Spread into five 13" x 9" baking pans, or cookie sheets with sides. Bake 20 to 30 minutes, stirring occasionally. Bake 15 minutes longer for crunchier texture. Cool. Add raisins or other dried fruit, if desired. Put in airtight containers. Label with date and contents. Store in a cool, dry place. Use within 6 months. Makes about 20 cups of CRUNCHY GRANOLA MIX.

1. Oats, wheat germ, coconut, sunflower, sesame seeds and chopped nuts are among the healthful ingredients to include in granola.

2. Pour the syrup of honey, molasses and brown sugar over the dry ingredients and stir to coat well.

Russian Refresher Mix

An imitation Russian tea—without the tea!

2 cups powdered orange drink
 mix
1 (3-oz.) pkg. presweetened
 powdered lemonade mix
1-1/3 cups sugar
1 teaspoon ground cinnamon
1/2 teaspoon ground cloves

Combine all ingredients in a medium bowl. Mix well. Put in a 1-quart air-tight container. Label with date and contents. Store in a cool, dry place. Use within 6 months. Makes about 3-1/2 cups RUSSIAN REFRESHER MIX.

Russian Refresher

Add 2 to 3 teaspoons of RUSSIAN REFRESHER MIX, see above, to 1 cup hot water. Stir to dissolve. Makes 1 serving.

Hot Chocolate Mix

The camper's favorite.

1 (25.6-oz.) pkg. instant nonfat
 dry milk (10-2/3 cups)
1 (6-oz.) jar powdered non-dairy
 creamer
2 cups powdered sugar
1 (6-oz.) can instant chocolate
 drink mix

Combine all ingredients in a large bowl. Mix well. Put in a large airtight container. Label with date and contents. Store in a cool, dry place. Use within 6 months. Makes about 17 cups HOT CHOCOLATE MIX.

Variation
Substitute 2 cups unsweetened cocoa powder for chocolate drink mix. Increase powdered sugar to 4 cups.

Hot Chocolate

Add 3 tablespoons HOT CHOCOLATE MIX, see above, to 1 cup hot water. Stir to dissolve. Makes 1 serving.

Orange Float Mix

A frothy, refreshing delight!

4 cups instant nonfat dry milk
2 cups powdered orange drink
   mix
1 cup sugar

Combine ingredients in a large bowl. Blend well. Put in a large airtight container. Label with date and contents. Store in a cool, dry place. Use within 6 months. Makes about 7 cups ORANGE FLOAT MIX.

Orange Float

Add 1 egg and 1/2 cup of ORANGE FLOAT MIX, see above, to 8 ounces of cold water in blender. Add 2 to 3 ice cubes and blend well. Serve immediately. Makes 1 serving.

Marie's Fruit Cocktail Mix

When summer fruits are at their peak, prepare this mix for future use.

4 cups sugar
2 qts. water
1 (6-oz.) can frozen orange juice
   concentrate
1 (6-oz.) can frozen lemonade
   concentrate
1 watermelon, cut in balls
2 cantaloupes, cut in chunks
2 crenshaw melons, cut in
   chunks
3 lbs. green grapes
3 lbs. peaches, cut in chunks
1 lb. blueberries, fresh or frozen

In a large saucepan bring sugar and water to a boil, stirring constantly. Stir in frozen orange juice concentrate and frozen lemonade concentrate. In a large bowl combine watermelon, cantaloupes, crenshaw melons, grapes, peaches and blueberries. Put mixed fruit in twelve 1-pint freezer containers, leaving 1/2-inch space at top. Pour hot juice syrup over top. Seal and label containers with date and contents. Freeze. Use within 6 to 8 months. Makes about 12 pints MARIE'S FRUIT COCKTAIL MIX.

Marie's Fruit Cocktail

Partially thaw 1 pint of MARIE'S FRUIT COCKTAIL MIX, see above. Spoon into fruit cups. Pour ginger ale over top, if desired. Makes 4 servings.

Fruit Slush Mix

A quick, cool, refreshing drink—right from your freezer.

4 cups sugar
4 cups water
1 (6-oz.) can frozen orange juice
   concentrate
1/2 cup lemon juice
1 (46-oz.) can pineapple juice

Combine sugar and water in a medium saucepan. Heat until sugar is dissolved. Add orange juice concentrate, lemon juice and pineapple juice. Fill 6 or 7 ice cube trays with mixture. Freeze until firm. Remove cubes from freezer trays and store in freezer bags. Label with date and contents. Use within 6 months. Makes about 100 small cubes.

Variation
Add 5 to 6 mashed bananas to mixture before freezing.

Fruit Slush

Fill a glass with FRUIT SLUSH MIX cubes, see above. Add ginger ale to cover. Let stand 15 minutes. Stir and serve. Makes 1 serving.

Meat Loaf Mix

For extra nutritional value, add 1 to 2 cups finely diced vegetables to mix (carrots, green peppers or celery).

3 eggs beaten
1 (8-oz.) can tomato sauce
1/4 cup dried chopped onion
1 tablespoon salt
2 tablespoons Worcestershire
   sauce
5 lbs. lean ground beef
1-1/2 cups rolled oats or bread
   crumbs

In a large bowl, combine eggs, tomato sauce, onion, salt and Worcestershire sauce. Stir in ground beef and rolled oats or bread crumbs. Cut three to four 15" x 12" pieces of plastic wrap or heavy-duty foil. Divide meat loaf mixture into three to four equal portions. Shape each portion into a meat loaf. Place on plastic wrap or heavy-duty foil. Wrap each meat loaf airtight. Label with date and contents. Store in freezer. Use within 3 months. Makes 3 to 4 packages MEAT LOAF MIX. To bake 1 meat loaf: Thaw meat loaf mixture. Lightly grease one 9" x 5" or one 7" x 3" loaf pan. Put meat loaf mixture into prepared pan. Preheat oven to 350F (175C). Bake for 1 hour or until done.

Cheese-Filled Lasagna or Manicotti Rolls

These are a real asset in your freezer. You can bank on it.

2 (16-oz.) pkgs. curly edged
   lasagna noodles or 2 (8-oz.)
   pkgs. manicotti shells
1 (10-oz.) pkg. frozen chopped
   spinach
1 (32-oz.) container ricotta
   cheese
4 eggs, beaten
1 cup grated Parmesan cheese
   (3-oz.)
2 tablespoons dried parsley
   flakes
1 teaspoon salt
1 teaspoon basil leaves, crushed
8 cups shredded mozzarella
   cheese (2 lbs.)

Cook lasagna or manicotti noodles according to package directions. Drain. Put in cold water while preparing filling. Cook spinach according to package directions. Drain well. In a large bowl, combine drained spinach, ricotta cheese, eggs, Parmesan cheese, parsley flakes, salt and basil. Mix well. Add mozzarella cheese and mix until well blended. Lay lasagna noodles or manicotti noodles on counter covered with plastic wrap. Pat dry with paper towels. Spread each lasagna noodle with 1/4 cup cheese mixture to within 1-inch of one end. Roll up firmly towards unfilled end. Continue with remaining noodles. Wrap each roll in plastic wrap and freeze. If using manicotti, fill each cooked tube with 1/3 cup cheese mixture. Wrap in plastic wrap and freeze. Makes 40 lasagna rolls or 28 manicotti rolls. To prepare 1 serving: Unwrap lasagna roll or manicotti roll and place in microwave bowl. Cover. Microwave on high for 1 to 2 minutes or until cheese begins to melt at ends of roll. Spoon 1/4 cup ITALIAN-STYLE MEAT MIX, page 26, or any prepared spaghetti sauce over roll; cover. Microwave on high for 20 to 30 seconds or until thoroughly heated. To prepare 8 servings: Place about 1/2 cup spaghetti sauce in the bottom of a 9-inch baking pan. Add 8 thawed, unwrapped lasagna or manicotti rolls. Cover with 1-1/2 cups more spaghetti sauce. Bake at 350F (175C) for 50 to 60 minutes or until heated through.

Slice and Bake Sugar Cookies

For a special treat, frost these cookies with Vanilla Buttercream Frosting.

2 cups butter or margarine,
  softened
2 cups granulated sugar
3 eggs
2 teaspoons vanilla extract
1 teaspoon lemon extract
6 cups all-purpose flour
1 teaspoon baking soda

Cut four 14" x 12" pieces of waxed paper or plastic wrap; set aside. In a large bowl, cream butter or margarine and sugar. Beat in eggs, vanilla and lemon extract until light and fluffy. In a large bowl, combine flour and baking soda. Gradually stir flour mixture into egg mixture until blended. Divide dough into 4 equal pieces. Shape each piece into an 8- to 10-inch roll. Wrap each roll in 1 piece of waxed paper or plastic wrap. Place wrapped rolls in a plastic freezer container with a tight-fitting lid, or wrap airtight in a 14" x 12" piece of heavy-duty foil; label. Store in freezer. Use within 6 months. Makes 4 rolls of dough or about 12 dozen cookies.

To bake 1 roll of dough: Preheat oven to 350F (175C). Lightly grease 2 large baking sheets. Cut frozen dough into 1/4-inch slices. Place slices on prepared baking sheets about 1/2 inch apart. Sprinkle slices lightly with granulated sugar, if desired. Bake 8 to 10 minutes until edges start to brown. Remove cookies from baking sheets. Cool on wire racks. Makes about 36 cookies.

SLICE AND BAKE SUGAR COOKIES makes:
Cookie Crust Fruit Tart, page 171

1. Slightly dampen hands. Shape dough into four 8- to 10-inch rolls. Wrap in waxed paper or plastic wrap.

2. Place wrapped rolls in freezer container or wrap airtight in heavy-duty foil. Label; freeze.

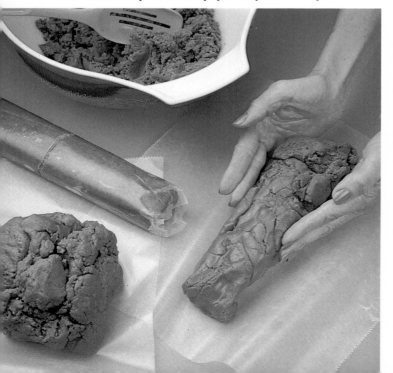

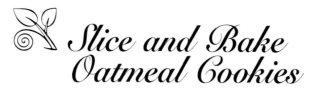

Slice and Bake Oatmeal Cookies

Chocolate chips are a nice addition to this cookie, either in place of the raisins or in addition to the raisins.

2 cups butter or margarine
2 cups granulated sugar
2 cups brown sugar, firmly
    packed
4 eggs
2 teaspoons vanilla extract
4 cups all-purpose flour
5 cups rolled oats, uncooked
1 teaspoon salt
2 teaspoons baking soda
2 teaspoons baking powder
3/4 cup chopped nuts
1 to 2 cups raisins

Cut four 14" x 12" pieces of waxed paper or plastic wrap. Cream butter or margarine, granulated sugar and brown sugar in a large bowl until smooth. Beat in eggs and vanilla until light and fluffy. In a medium bowl, combine flour, oats, salt, baking soda and baking powder. Gradually stir flour mixture into egg mixture until blended. Stir in nuts and raisins. Divide dough into 4 equal pieces. Shape each piece into an 8- to 10-inch roll. Wrap each roll in 1 piece of waxed paper or plastic wrap. Place wrapped rolls in a plastic freezer container with a tight-fitting lid, or wrap airtight in a 14" x 12" piece of heavy-duty foil. Label with date and contents. Store in freezer. Use within 6 months. Makes 4 rolls of dough or about 12 dozen cookies.

  To bake 1 roll of dough: Preheat oven to 375F (190C). Lightly grease 2 large baking sheets; set aside. Cut slightly thawed dough into 1/4-inch slices. Place slices about 1 inch apart on prepared baking sheets. Bake 10 to 12 minutes until edges are light brown and centers are slightly set. Cool about 2 minutes on baking sheet. Remove cookies from baking sheets. Cool completely on wire racks. Makes about 36 cookies.

Crumb Topping Mix

This topping is tops!

1-1/3 cups brown sugar, firmly
    packed
1 cup all-purpose flour
2 teaspoons ground cinnamon
1/2 teaspoon ground nutmeg
3/4 cup butter or margarine

In a medium bowl, combine brown sugar, flour and cinnamon. Mix well. With a pastry blender, cut in butter or margarine until mixture is very fine. Put in a 1-quart, airtight container. Label with date and contents. Store in the refrigerator. Use within 1 to 2 months. Makes about 2 cups of CRUMB TOPPING MIX.

CRUMB TOPPING MIX makes:
Topping on cobblers, fruit pies, puddings, ice cream and fruit cups

Slice and Bake
Peanut Butter Cookies

Use a wire whisk to stir the flour and baking soda together.

2 cups vegetable shortening
2 cups granulated sugar
2 cups brown sugar, firmly
    packed
2 cups creamy or chunk-style
    peanut butter
2 teaspoons vanilla extract
4 eggs
5 cups all-purpose flour
4 teaspoons baking soda

Cut four 14" x 12" pieces of waxed paper or plastic wrap; set aside. Cream shortening, granulated sugar, brown sugar and peanut butter in a large bowl. Beat in vanilla and eggs until light and fluffy. In a large bowl, combine flour and baking soda. Gradually stir flour mixture into egg mixture until blended. Divide dough into 4 equal pieces. Shape each piece into an 8- to 10-inch roll. Wrap each roll in 1 piece of waxed paper or plastic wrap. Place wrapped rolls in a plastic freezer container with a tight-fitting lid, or wrap airtight in a 14" x 12" piece of heavy-duty foil. Label with date and contents. Store in freezer. Use within 6 months. Makes 4 rolls dough or about 12 dozen cookies.

To bake 1 roll of dough: Let dough thaw slightly. Preheat oven to 350F (175C). Cut slightly thawed dough into 1-inch thick slices. Cut each slice into fourths. Roll each piece into a ball. Place balls on an ungreased baking sheet about 1-1/2 inches apart. Use tines of a fork to flatten cookies by pressing down in crisscross fashion. Bake 8 to 10 minutes until lightly browned around edges. Remove from baking sheet. Cool on wire racks. Makes about 36 cookies.

SLICE AND BAKE PEANUT BUTTER COOKIES makes:
Mini-Peanut Butter and Chocolate Cookies, page 171

Slice and Bake Chocolate Chip Cookies

It will be easier to shape the rolls of dough if you wet your hands.

2 cups butter or margarine
1-1/3 cups granulated sugar
1-2/3 cups brown sugar, firmly
   packed
1 tablespoon vanilla extract
4 eggs
5-1/2 cups all purpose flour
2 teaspoons salt
2 teaspoons baking soda
2 cups semisweet chocolate chips
1 cup chopped nuts

Cut four 14" x 12" pieces of waxed paper or plastic wrap; set aside. In a large bowl, cream butter or margarine, granulated sugar and brown sugar. Beat in vanilla and eggs until light and fluffy. In a large bowl, combine flour, salt and baking soda. Gradually stir flour mixture into egg mixture until blended. Stir in chocolate chips and nuts. Divide dough into 4 equal pieces. Shape each piece into an 8- to 10-inch roll. Wrap each roll in 1 piece of waxed paper or plastic wrap. Place wrapped rolls in a plastic freezer container with a tight-fitting lid, or wrap airtight in a 14" x 12" piece of heavy-duty foil. Label with date and contents. Store in freezer. Use within 6 months. Makes 4 rolls of dough or about 12 dozen cookies.

To bake 1 roll of dough: Preheat oven to 350F (175C). Cut slightly frozen dough into 1/4-inch slices. Arrange cut pieces on an ungreased baking sheet about 1-1/2 inches apart. Bake 10 minutes until lightly browned around edges. Remove cookies from baking sheets. Cool on wire racks. Makes about 36 cookies.

Appetizers and Snacks

Because appetizers are supposed to be just tasty morsels that tantalize the appetite before a meal, you may not want to spend a long time preparing them when you'd rather visit with your guests. Get out your mixes! You can dream up lots of ideas for appetizers as you read through this book. Among the Special Mixes you'll find some delicious chip and dips. Be sure to try QUICK TACO DIP, page 52.

MARIE'S FRUIT COCKTAIL, page 43, is a refreshing taste for any hot, summer day. So is the FRUIT SLUSH MIX, page 44.

Fried appetizers should be served hot. They wilt and are not as appealing when cold. Won Tons and Mini Chimis can be served as the first course of a meal or as finger foods for a buffet table. They can both be prepared ahead and frozen. They can be crisped and reheated for 1-minute at 400F (205C) right before serving.

Serve appetizers attractively, arranging tasty tidbits on small platters which can be easily replaced or replenished. Large trays soon lose their neat appearance. Simple, colorful garnishes on the trays will add to their eye appeal. Vary the types of appetizers served at a buffet table, combining one or two hot ones with several cold dishes. Offer your guests crisp vegetables along with a selection of CREAMY CRUDITÉ DIP and HOME-STYLE DIP.

Curried Shrimp Rounds

Here's a unique flavor combination you can't resist.

3 cups QUICK MIX, page 11
2/3 cup milk or water
2 (4-1/2-oz.) cans shrimp,
    drained and rinsed
1 cup shredded Swiss cheese (4
    oz.)
1/2 cup mayonnaise
2 tablespoons finely chopped
    green onion
1 tablespoon lemon juice
1/4 teaspoon curry powder
1/2 cup thinly sliced water
    chestnuts
Parsley flakes, for garnish

Preheat oven to 400F (205C). Grease 2 baking sheets. In a medium bowl, combine QUICK MIX and milk or water. Stir until blended. Let dough stand 5 minutes. On a lightly floured board, knead dough about 15 times. Roll out dough to 1/8-inch thickness. Cut with a small floured cookie cutter and place biscuits on prepared baking sheets. In a small bowl, combine shrimp, Swiss cheese, mayonnaise, onion, lemon juice and curry powder. Spoon shrimp mixture onto biscuits. Top with water chestnuts and sprinkle with parsley. Bake 10 to 12 minutes. Makes about 40 appetizers.

Big Soft Pretzels

Try these with a cool drink for a great snack.

1 tablespoon active dry yeast
    (1 (1/4-oz.) package)
1-1/2 cups lukewarm water
    (110F, 45C)
2 eggs, beaten
1/2 cup vegetable oil or melted
    margarine
5 to 6 cups HOT ROLL MIX,
    page 12
1 egg, beaten
About 2 tablespoons coarse salt

Lightly grease 2 large baking sheets. In a large bowl, dissolve yeast in lukewarm water. Blend in 2 eggs and oil or margarine. Add 5 cups HOT ROLL MIX. Stir well. Add additional HOT ROLL MIX to make a soft, but not too sticky dough. Knead about 5 minutes, until dough is smooth. Roll pieces of dough into ropes about 1/2 inch in diameter and 18 to 24 inches long. Form into pretzel shapes. For pretzel sticks, cut dough into 5- to 6-inch lengths. Place on prepared baking sheets. Preheat oven to 425F (220C). Brush tops of pretzels with beaten egg and sprinkle with coarse salt. Bake immediately 12 to 15 minutes, until brown and crisp. Makes 12 to 15 large pretzels.

Variation
For a chewier pretzel, drop pretzel-shaped dough into a pan of boiling water. When dough floats to the top of the water, remove it. Preheat oven to 400F (205C). Brush with egg and sprinkle with coarse salt. Bake about 30 minutes.

Quick Taco Dip

Make this a day ahead, then just heat it and serve with corn chips!

2 cups ALL-PURPOSE
   GROUND BEEF MIX, page
   29, thawed
1/2 cup ketchup
1 tablespoon chili powder
2 (15-oz.) cans kidney beans
1/4 to 1/2 teaspoon hot pepper
   sauce
1 cup shredded Cheddar cheese
   (4 oz.)
1/2 cup sliced green olives with
   pimientos, for garnish

In a large saucepan, combine ALL-PURPOSE GROUND BEEF MIX, ketchup and chili powder. Mash kidney beans and add with bean juice to meat mixture. Add hot pepper sauce. Heat through about 10 minutes. Put in a chafing dish and top with shredded Cheddar cheese. Garnish with green olives. Makes about 6 cups dip, enough for 15 to 20 servings.

Cheese Fondue

With fondue this easy to make, you'll be tempted to serve it every day.

3 cups FREEZER CHEESE
   SAUCE MIX, page 23,
   thawed
1/4 teaspoon dry mustard
Pinch garlic powder
1 (1-lb.) loaf French bread, cut
   in 1-inch cubes
2 red Delicious apples, sliced, if
   desired

In a medium saucepan, combine FREEZER CHEESE SAUCE MIX, dry mustard and garlic powder. Stir until heated through. Pour into a warm fondue pot. Serve with French bread cubes and apple slices, if desired. Makes 8 to 10 servings.

Speedy Pizza

Teenagers eat these by the dozens.

2 cups MEAT SAUCE MIX,
    page 24, thawed
6 English muffins, split
Oregano, for garnish
1 cup shredded mozzarella
    cheese (4 oz.)
Pepperoni, mushrooms, green
    peppers and olives, as desired

In a small saucepan, simmer MEAT SAUCE MIX about 5 minutes, until heated through. Toast English muffin halves. Spoon meat mixture generously over English muffins. Sprinkle with oregano and top with grated mozzarella cheese. Add toppings as desired. Broil about 3 to 5 minutes, until cheese is bubbly. Makes 12 individual pizzas.

Cocktail Meatballs

Place this casserole in your microwave oven and heat it 5 minutes.

2 tablespoons butter or
    margarine
1/3 cup chopped green pepper
1/3 cup chopped onion
1 (10-3/4-oz.) can condensed
    tomato soup
2 tablespoons brown sugar,
    firmly packed
4 teaspoons Worcestershire sauce
1 tablespoon prepared mustard
1 tablespoon vinegar
1 container MEATBALL MIX,
    page 25, thawed (about 30
    meatballs)

Preheat oven to 350F (175C). Melt butter or margarine in a small saucepan. Sauté green pepper and onion in butter or margarine until tender. In a 2-quart casserole, combine tomato soup, brown sugar, Worcestershire sauce, mustard and vinegar. Add sautéed green pepper and onion. Stir in MEATBALL MIX. Bake about 20 minutes, until heated through. Keep warm. Serve meatballs on toothpicks. Makes about 30 appetizers.

Mini-Chimis

Serve on a party buffet with guacamole and green chili salsa.

Vegetable oil for frying
4 cups MEXICAN MEAT MIX,
  page 27, thawed
2 (16-oz.) pkgs. won-ton skins

In a large skillet, heat 2 inches of oil to 375F (190C) or until a 1-inch bread cube turns golden brown in about 50 seconds. Place 1 heaping teaspoonful of the meat mixture in lower corner of each won-ton skin. Fold point of won-ton skin up over filling, then fold side corners in. Moisten top corner with water and roll skin into a cylinder. Repeat with remaining meat filling. Lower several rolls at a time into hot oil. Fry 3 to 4 minutes or until golden brown, turning if necessary to brown evenly. Drain on paper towels. If preparing ahead, cool, then arrange in a single layer in freezer containers. Cover tightly and freeze up to 3 months. To serve, thaw and place in a single layer on large baking sheets. Preheat oven to 375F (190C); bake rolls 10 to 15 minutes or until crisp, turning once. Makes 120 mini-chimis.

 *Won Tons*

Serve these won tons at your next buffet dinner.

Sweet and Sour Sauce, see
   below
2 cups CUBED PORK MIX,
   page 28, thawed
1/4 teaspoon freshly grated
   gingerroot
2 tablespoons finely sliced green
   onion
2 teaspoons soy sauce
1 (16-oz.) pkg. won-ton skins
Oil for deep-frying

Sweet and Sour Sauce:
2 tablespoons cornstarch
1-1/4 cups pineapple juice
2 tablespoons white vinegar
1/3 cup brown sugar, firmly
   packed
1/4 cup ketchup
1 tablespoon soy sauce

Prepare Sweet and Sour Sauce; keep warm. Shred meat from CUBED PORK MIX with 2 forks. In a medium bowl, combine shredded meat, remaining mix, gingerroot, onion and soy sauce. Place about 1 teaspoon pork mixture in center of each won-ton skin. Moisten edges with water. Bring opposite corners together to make a triangle. Seal by pressing edges firmly with your fingers. Pour oil about 2 inches deep in a deep fryer or medium saucepan. Heat oil to 375F (190C). With a slotted spoon, carefully lower filled won tons into hot oil. Cook about 30 seconds on each side until crisp and golden brown. Drain on paper towels. To serve, dip won tons into sauce. Makes about 36 won tons.

Sweet and Sour Sauce

In a medium saucepan, combine cornstarch and 1/4 cup pineapple juice until smooth. Stir in remaining ingredients. Cook and stir over medium heat until smooth and slightly thickened.

1. Remove meat cubes from mix. Shred meat by pulling apart with 2 forks.

2. Spoon filling onto skins. Moisten edges. Fold diagonally; pinch edges to seal.

Soups, Sauces and Salad Dressings

Our soups are great "tummy warmers" for the winter months. Most can be prepared ahead and reheated in a jiffy. Best-Ever Minestrone, Broccoli-Cheese Soup and Hearty New England Clam Chowder make frequent appearances at the table. A salad and hot bread add the finishing touches to this "down home" meal.

Learn to master basic white sauce and all its variations with WHITE SAUCE MIX. Be creative in preparing your own homemade soups and sauces with it. WHITE SAUCE MIX is one of the few mixes that requires refrigeration for storage.

Prepare our Trio of Dressings so you'll always be prepared to toss together a superb green side salad or main dish salad on a moment's notice. Our Peppercream Dressing is our favorite and can be used in a variety of ways. Be sure to give this one a try!

Trio of Dressings

This "trio" in your refrigerator will bring you a "chorus" of praises.

1/2 cup granulated sugar
1/2 cup vegetable oil
1/2 cup ketchup
1/2 cup cider vinegar

French Dressing

Combine all ingredients in blender or food processor. Blend 30 seconds. Pour into pint jar. Cover and store in refrigerator. Use within 1 month. Makes about 2 cups French Dressing.

Favorite Use for French Dressing
Fresh Spinach Salad: Combine fresh, torn spinach leaves with chopped hard-cooked egg and crisp bacon pieces. Top with French Dressing just before serving.

1 cup mayonnaise
4 tablespoons milk
1 tablespoon freshly grated
    Parmesan cheese
1 teaspoon pepper
1 teaspoon rice vinegar
1 teaspoon lemon juice
1 green onion, minced
1/2 teaspoon garlic salt
2 drops hot pepper sauce
2 drops Worcestershire sauce

Peppercream Dressing

Combine all ingredients in blender or food processor. Blend 30 seconds. Pour into pint jar. Cover and store in refrigerator. Use within 1 month. Makes about 1-1/3 cups Peppercream Dressing.

Favorite Use for Peppercream Dressing
Red Potato Salad: Combine small red, cooked potatoes, quartered, with sliced radishes and chopped green onions. Toss together; chill before serving.

1 cup granulated sugar
1/2 teaspoon salt
1/2 cup cider vinegar
2 tablespoons minced onion or 2
    tablespoons dried onion
    flakes
2 tablespoons poppy seeds
1-1/4 cups vegetable oil

Poppy Seed Dressing

Combine all ingredients in blender or food processor. Blend 30 seconds. Pour into pint jar. Cover and store in refrigerator. Use within 1 month.

Favorite Use for Poppy Seed Dressing
Mandarin Chicken Salad: Combine tossed salad greens, drained mandarin oranges, sliced red Bermuda onion and diced cooked chicken. Toss with Poppy Seed Dressing. Just before serving top with chow mein noodles.

Basic White Sauce

Acquaint yourself with this family of sauces.

1/2 cup WHITE SAUCE MIX,
    page 22
1 cup cool water
Pepper, herbs and spices, if
    desired

In a small saucepan, combine WHITE SAUCE MIX and water. For thinner sauce, decrease WHITE SAUCE MIX to 1/4 cup. For thick sauce, increase WHITE SAUCE MIX to 3/4 cup. Cook over low heat until smooth, stirring constantly. Season with pepper, herbs and spices, if desired. Makes about 1-1/2 cups sauce.

Variations
Substitute milk, tomato juice or chicken or beef stock for all or part of water.

Cheese Sauce: Add 1/2 to 1 cup shredded Cheddar cheese after mixture thickens. Stir until cheese is melted.

Curry Sauce: Add 1 teaspoon curry powder to thickened mixture.

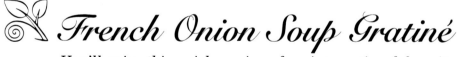

French Onion Soup Gratiné

You'll enjoy this quick version of an international favorite.

2 pkgs. ONION SEASONING
    MIX, page 18
4 cups water or beef broth
1/4 cup butter or margarine,
    softened
6 slices French bread, 1 inch
    thick
3 cups shredded Swiss cheese
    (12 oz)
2 tablespoons grated Parmesan
    cheese

In a large saucepan, combine ONION SEASONING MIX and water or broth. Bring to a boil over medium-high heat. Simmer over low heat about 10 minutes. Preheat oven to 375F (190C). Spread butter or margarine evenly on 1 side of bread slices. Arrange buttered bread slices on an ungreased baking sheet. Toast bread in oven until browned and quite dry, about 10 minutes. Remove from oven. Sprinkle about 2 tablespoons Swiss cheese on each toasted bread slice. Return bread to oven until cheese melts. Divide remaining Swiss cheese evenly in 6 soup bowls. Pour soup into bowls. Float 1 bread slice on top of each. Sprinkle evenly with Parmesan cheese. Makes 6 servings.

Hearty New England Clam Chowder

The tantalizing aroma of this chowder says, "Welcome home."

2 (6-1/2-oz.) cans minced clams
1 cup finely chopped onions
1 cup finely chopped celery
2 cups pared and diced potatoes
Water
1-1/2 cups WHITE SAUCE
   MIX, page 22
1 quart milk
1/2 teaspoon sugar
Salt and pepper to taste

Drain clams, reserving juice. In a large saucepan, combine clam juice, onions, celery and potatoes. Add enough water to just cover vegetables. Cook over medium heat about 15 minutes until tender.

While vegetables are cooking, combine WHITE SAUCE MIX and milk in a large kettle or Dutch oven. Cook over low heat until thick and smooth, stirring constantly. Add clams, undrained vegetables and sugar. Heat through about 15 minutes. Add salt and pepper to taste. Makes 6 servings.

Broccoli Cheese Soup in Bread Bowls

Most supermarket bakeries will make these bread loaves for you, if you can't find them on the shelves.

1-1/2 lbs. fresh broccoli, chopped
   (about 3 cups)
2 potatoes, peeled and diced
1 carrot, peeled and diced
1 onion, chopped
4 cups chicken broth
1-1/2 cups WHITE SAUCE
   MIX, page 22
1-1/2 cups milk
1 cup shredded Cheddar cheese
   (4 oz.)
1/4 teaspoon ground nutmeg, if
   desired
Salt and pepper to taste
6 large (3-oz.) round hard rolls

In a large 4-quart saucepan, put prepared broccoli, potatoes, carrots and onion. Add chicken broth to cover vegetables. Cook over medium heat 15 to 20 minutes until vegetables are almost tender. In medium bowl, combine WHITE SAUCE MIX and milk. Add mixture to cooked vegetables, stirring constantly 2 to 3 minutes until thickened. Stir in cheese until melted. Add nutmeg, salt and pepper to taste. Slice tops off of rolls. Scoop out soft bread from inside of roll leaving crusty shell. Spoon soup into bread bowls. Replace top of bread or serve to the side of soup. Makes about 2 quarts soup or 6 large servings.

Variation
Scooped out bread bowls can be lightly toasted in oven, if desired, before filling with soup.

1. *Cook thinly sliced onions in bacon drippings until light brown. Add potatoes and enough water to cover. Cook over medium heat 10 to 15 minutes.*

2. *Combine 2 cups milk, and WHITE SAUCE MIX in a saucepan. Cook until thick and smooth, stirring constantly. Stir in cream-style corn, salt and pepper.*

3. *Add white sauce and corn mixture to potatoes and heat through.*

4. *Serve in soup bowls. Top each serving with crumbled bacon and butter or margarine.*

Cream of Chicken Soup

Perfect on a cold winter day!

2 chicken bouillon cubes
2 cups hot water
1-1/2 cups WHITE SAUCE
   MIX, page 22
1 cup minced, cooked chicken
1/2 cup finely chopped celery
1/2 cup finely chopped onion
1/2 teaspoon salt
1 teaspoon garlic salt
4 cups milk
1 egg yolk, beaten
Chopped chives or watercress,
   for garnish

Dissolve chicken bouillon cubes in hot water. Combine WHITE SAUCE MIX and bouillon mixture in a large kettle or Dutch oven. Cook over low heat about 5 minutes, stirring constantly, until thick and smooth. Add chicken, celery, onion, salt and garlic salt. Simmer 15 minutes, stirring constantly. Blend in milk and egg yolk. Simmer 5 more minutes. Remove from heat. Garnish with chopped chives or watercress. Makes 6 servings.

Eastern Corn Chowder

A crisp salad with crackers completes this meal.

5 slices bacon
1 medium onion, thinly sliced
2 medium potatoes, pared and
   diced
Water
2 cups milk
1 cup WHITE SAUCE MIX,
   page 22
1 (17-oz.) can cream-style corn
1 teaspoon salt
Dash of pepper
1 tablespoon butter or
   margarine, for garnish

In a large frying pan, cook bacon until crisp. Crumble and set aside. Reserve 3 tablespoons bacon drippings in pan. Add onion and cook until light brown. Add potatoes and enough water to cover. Cook over medium heat 10 to 15 minutes, until potatoes are cooked. Combine milk and WHITE SAUCE MIX in a small saucepan. Cook over low heat until thick and smooth, stirring constantly. Stir in cream-style corn, salt and pepper. Add to potato mixture and heat through about 10 minutes. Top each serving with crumbled bacon and butter or margarine. Makes 6 servings.

Pork Noodles

Linguine is also known as flat spaghetti.

1-1/2 cups water
1-1/2 teaspoons instant chicken
  bouillon granules
2 cups CUBED PORK MIX,
  page 28, thawed
1-1/2 teaspoons soy sauce
1 (8-oz.) pkg. linguine
3 hard-cooked eggs, sliced, for
  garnish
3 chopped green onions, for
  garnish

In a medium saucepan, bring water to a boil. Add bouillon granules; stir until dissolved. Stir in CUBED PORK MIX and soy sauce. Bring to a boil. Simmer about 5 minutes over low heat, stirring occasionally. Cook linguine according to package directions. Spoon cooked linguine evenly into 4 soup bowls. Pour pork mixture evenly over top of each. Garnish each with hard-cooked egg slices and chopped green onions. Makes 4 servings.

Best-Ever Minestrone Soup

This is our favorite soup!

1 (28-oz.) can tomatoes
2 cups ALL-PURPOSE
  GROUND BEEF MIX, page
  29, thawed
1 quart water
2 large carrots, peeled, sliced
2 (8-oz.) cans tomato sauce
2 cups beef broth
1 tablespoon dried parsley leaves
1/2 teaspoon basil leaves
1 teaspoon dried oregano leaves
1/4 teaspoon pepper
1/2 teaspoon garlic salt
1 (15-oz.) can garbanzo beans,
  drained
1 (16-oz.) can green beans,
  drained
1 (15-oz.) can kidney beans,
  drained
1-1/4 cups mostaccioli macaroni,
  uncooked
Parmesan cheese, for garnish

Puree tomatoes in blender. In a large pot or Dutch oven, combine ALL-PURPOSE GROUND BEEF MIX, pureed tomatoes, water, carrots, tomato sauce, broth, parsley, basil, oregano, pepper and garlic salt. Bring to a boil. Cover; simmer over low heat about 20 minutes. Add garbanzo beans, green beans and kidney beans. Bring to a boil; add macaroni. Cook 10 to 12 minutes until macaroni is tender. Garnish with Parmesan cheese. Makes 10 to 12 servings.

Best-Ever Minestrone Soup

Zucchini Casserole

A perfect accompaniment to any meat dish. Or serve it as a main dish!

4 medium zucchini, sliced 1/2
   inch thick
3/4 cup pared and sliced carrots
Water, salted
1/2 cup chopped onion
6 tablespoons butter or
   margarine
2-1/4 cups HERBED
   STUFFING MIX, page 17
1 (10-3/4-oz.) can cream of
   chicken soup
1/2 cup dairy sour cream

In a medium saucepan, put zucchini and carrots in enough boiling, salted water to cover them. Cover pan and simmer about 15 minutes, until vegetables are tender. Drain. In a large saucepan, sauté onion in 4 tablespoons of the butter or margarine until tender. Stir in 1-1/2 cups of the HERBED STUFFING MIX, cream of chicken soup and sour cream. Gently stir in zucchini. Preheat oven to 350F (175C). Lightly butter a 1-1/2-quart casserole. Put mixture into casserole. Melt remaining butter or margarine in a small saucepan. Add remaining HERBED STUFFING MIX to butter or margarine. Toss gently and sprinkle over casserole. Bake 30 to 40 minutes. Makes 6 to 8 servings.

Variation
Chicken-Zucchini Casserole: Add 1 package CHICKEN MIX, page 30, or 2 cups cooked, diced chicken.

Green Peppers Italian-Style

For exceptional flavor, use 1/2 pound fresh mushrooms in this delightful side dish.

3 tablespoons vegetable oil
4 large green peppers, cut in
   thin strips
1/2 teaspoon onion salt
1/4 teaspoon pepper
2 (4-oz.) cans mushrooms,
   drained
1/2 cup ITALIAN-STYLE
   MEAT MIX, page 26, thawed

Heat oil in a large skillet. Add green pepper strips, onion salt and pepper. Stirring occasionally, sauté over medium-high heat until peppers are crisp-tender, about 3 minutes. Stir in mushrooms and ITALIAN-STYLE MEAT MIX. Simmer over low heat until heated through, 15 to 20 minutes. Makes 6 to 8 servings.

Main Dishes

Do you hate that last-minute frenzy when you are trying to put a meal together and everyone is hungry and in a hurry? Be ready by having these skip-a-step mixes on hand to trim your preparation time to minutes.

The secret comes in planning ahead. It's easy to prepare several mixes when you have the time, then use them when you're in a hurry.

ALL-PURPOSE GROUND BEEF MIX, page 29; ITALIAN-STYLE MEAT MIX, page 26; CHICKEN MIX, page 30; and MEXICAN MEAT MIX, page 27 are some of our favorites to have on hand to make our meal preparations and clean up time easier. The ALL-PURPOSE GROUND BEEF MIX and CHICKEN MIX can be substituted in all your recipes that call for one pound hamburger, browned and seasoned or 2 cups cooked, diced chicken. You've just eliminated the step of having to cook the meat and clean up the mess after each recipe by preparing for 5 or 6 recipes at one time.

If your family is on the go, you'll find the CHEESE-FILLED LASAGNA OR MANICOTTI ROLLS a convenient type of mix. These rolls are individual servings of lasagna or manicotti that can be used one at a time for the family member whose schedule conflicts with mealtime. Or you have the option of preparing enough to feed your family all at one time.

This section includes a variety of main dishes for any occasion. Hawaiian Haystack is a favorite for company—because of its eye appeal as well as ease of preparation. If you're in the mood for Mexican fare, our Chimichangas are the number one preference.

Convenience cooking with mixes would not be complete without stir frying. A new trend towards healthier cooking also makes this an ideal method. A wok is the appropriate cooking utensil, but you can use a heavy skillet. Prepare all the ingredients before heating the oil because there isn't enough time once you begin cooking. Nothing is more appetizing than tender, juicy, golden brown strips of meat and brightly colored vegetables cooked crisp-tender so their true flavor is released and texture is maintained. Stir-Fry Cashew Chicken and Teriyaki Beef and Vegetables use this cooking method, but you can use the ORIENTAL STIR-FRY MIX to create your own favorite combinations, too.

Chicken Oahu

The sauce is the star of this blend of flavors from the Islands.

4 cups HERBED STUFFING
    MIX, page 17
1 (8-oz.) can crushed pineapple,
    undrained
1/4 cup water
1/2 cup all-purpose flour
1/2 teaspoon salt
1/2 teaspoon paprika
Dash of pepper
1 (2-1/2- to 3-lb.) fryer chicken,
    cut up
Creamy Sauce, see below

Creamy Sauce:
1-1/2 cups chopped celery
1/2 cup chopped onion
2 tablespoons chopped green
    pepper
1/2 cup water
1 (10-3/4-oz.) can cream of
    mushroom soup
1/2 cup dairy sour cream
1 tablespoon soy sauce

Preheat oven to 375F (190C). Lightly grease a 13" x 9" baking dish. In a medium bowl, combine HERBED STUFFING MIX, pineapple and water. Put into prepared baking dish. In a plastic bag, combine flour, salt, paprika and dash of pepper. Add chicken pieces 2 at a time and shake to coat. Place chicken on top of stuffing mixture. Cover with foil. Bake 30 minutes. Remove foil and bake 30 more minutes. Prepare Creamy Sauce and spoon over top of chicken. Makes 6 servings.

Creamy Sauce

In a medium skillet, combine celery, onion, green pepper and water. Cover and simmer 10 minutes. Drain off water. Add soup, sour cream and soy sauce. Heat through.

Self-Crust Cheese Tart

Easiest pie for a light supper.

Paprika
1 cup shredded Swiss cheese (4
    oz.)
4 strips bacon, cooked and
    crumbled
3 eggs
1/4 teaspoon salt
1/4 teaspoon ground nutmeg, if
    desired
1-1/2 cups milk
1 teaspoon instant minced onion
1/3 cup QUICK MIX, page 11

Preheat oven to 325F (165C). Generously butter a 9-inch pie plate. Sprinkle bottom and sides of prepared pie plate lightly with paprika. Layer Swiss cheese and bacon on bottom of pie plate. Combine eggs, salt, nutmeg, milk, onion and QUICK MIX in a blender. Blend at medium speed about 1 minute, until thoroughly mixed. Pour over cheese and bacon in pie plate. Bake 30 to 40 minutes, until a toothpick inserted in center comes out clean. Serve hot. Makes 6 servings.

Impossible Pie

This pie forms its own custard on the bottom with a cake-like crust on top.

1/2 cup sugar
4 eggs
2 cups milk
1 teaspoon vanilla extract
3 tablespoons butter or
    margarine, melted
1/2 teaspoon ground cinnamon
1/4 teaspoon ground nutmeg
1/2 cup QUICK MIX, page 11

Preheat oven to 400F (205C). Butter a 9-inch pie plate. In a blender, combine sugar, eggs, milk, vanilla, melted butter or margarine, cinnamon and nutmeg. Blend until smooth. Add QUICK MIX and blend 30 more seconds. Pour into prepared pie pan. Bake 25 to 30 minutes, until golden. Cool on a wire rack. Serve warm. Makes one 9-inch pie.

Monte Cristo Sandwiches

Add some pizzazz to ham and cheese sandwiches.

12 slices white bread
Mayonnaise
12 thin slices natural Swiss
    cheese
6 thin slices baked ham
6 thin slices roast turkey
2 eggs, beaten
1 cup milk
1 cup BUTTERMILK
    PANCAKE AND WAFFLE
    MIX, page 13
Butter for griddle
Powdered sugar, for garnish
Currant jelly, for garnish

Preheat griddle to 350F (175C). Spread 1 side of each slice of bread with a thin coating of mayonnaise. Assemble each sandwich using 2 slices of Swiss cheese, 1 slice of ham and 1 slice of turkey. Trim crusts with a sharp knife, making the edges even. Cut each sandwich in half. Set aside. Combine eggs and milk in a shallow dish. Add BUTTERMILK PAN-CAKE AND WAFFLE MIX. Butter griddle. Dip each sandwich into the batter. Grill about 3 to 4 minutes, until lightly browned on both sides and cheese begins to melt. Lightly sprinkle with powdered sugar and currant jelly. Makes 6 sandwiches.

Variation
Omit turkey slices and use 12 slices of ham.

1. Assemble sandwiches with 2 slices of Swiss cheese, 1 slice of ham and 1 slice of turkey. Trim the crusts, making the edges even.

2. Dip each sandwich into the batter, then grill until lightly browned on both sides and cheese begins to melt.

3. Serve Monte Cristo Sandwiches sprinkled with powdered sugar and topped with currant jelly.

Bread Basket Stew

Believe it or not, the Bread Basket Bowls hold their shape until you start to eat them.

Bread Basket Bowls, see below
1 pkg. FIVE-WAY BEEF MIX
    made with cubed beef, page
    31, thawed
2 (8-oz.) cans tomato sauce
1 (17-oz.) can whole-kernel corn,
    undrained
2 cups sliced fresh mushrooms
    or 1 (8-oz.) can mushroom
    pieces, drained
1 tablespoon Worcestershire
    sauce
1 bay leaf, if desired

Bread Basket Bowls:
1 tablespoon active dry yeast
    (1 (1/4)-oz. package)
1-1/2 cups lukewarm water
    (110F, 45C)
1 egg, slightly beaten
2 tablespoons vegetable oil
About 5-1/2 cups HOT ROLL
    MIX, page 12
1 egg
1 tablespoon water

Prepare Bread Basket Bowls; set aside. In a medium sauce-pan, combine FIVE-WAY BEEF MIX, tomato sauce, corn, mushrooms, Worcestershire sauce and bay leaf, if desired. Bring to a boil over medium-high heat. Cover and simmer over low heat 25 minutes. Remove bay leaf. Place each Bread Basket Bowl on a plate. Ladle stew into bowls. Makes 6 to 8 servings.

Bread Basket Bowls

In a large bowl dissolve yeast in lukewarm water. When yeast bubbles, stir in 1 beaten egg and oil. Gradually stir in 3 cups HOT ROLL MIX until blended. Add enough additional HOT ROLL MIX to make a stiff dough. Turn out on a lightly floured surface. Knead until smooth, about 10 minutes. Add additional flour to surface as needed. Grease bowl. Place dough in greased bowl, turning to grease all sides. Cover and let rise in a warm place until doubled in bulk, about 1-1/2 hours. While dough is rising, generously grease the outsides and bottoms of eight 10-ounce custard cups; set aside. Punch down dough. Turn out on lightly floured surface. Knead about 5 times. Divide dough into 8 equal pieces. Shape pieces of dough into smooth balls. Use a rolling pin to roll out 1 ball into a 6-inch circle. Lay rolled-out dough over 1 inverted and greased custard cup. Mold dough circle to cover cup. Repeat with other balls of dough. Arrange dough-covered custard cups on 2 ungreased baking sheets, about 2 inches apart. Let stand uncovered 10 minutes. Preheat oven to 375F (190C). Bake bowls 20 minutes. Beat 1 egg with 1 tablespoon water. Remove custard cups from oven. Brush bread bowls with egg-water mixture. Bake 5 minutes longer. Remove from oven. Turn right side up; remove custard cups. Brush inside of each bread bowl with egg-water mixture. Bake 10 to 15 minutes longer until lightly browned inside and outside. Cool on a wire rack.

Chicken Strata

Give it a layered look!

1 (2-1/2- to 3-lb.) stewing
   chicken
1 carrot, pared and sliced
1 onion, sliced
2 teaspoons salt
2 qts. water
2 cups chicken broth
1/2 cup butter or margarine
1/2 cup all-purpose flour
1 teaspoon salt
1/2 cup milk
2 eggs, slightly beaten
3 cups HERBED STUFFING
   MIX, page 17
1 cup dry bread crumbs
1/4 cup butter or margarine,
   melted

In a large saucepan, combine chicken, carrot, onion, 2 teaspoons salt and water. Cover and cook over high heat about 5 minutes, until water boils. Reduce heat and simmer 1-1/2 to 2 hours, until chicken is tender. Remove from heat. Strain broth and refrigerate until fat can be skimmed from top. Cool chicken. Remove meat from bones, and discard bones and skin. Melt 1/2 cup butter or margarine in a medium saucepan. Stir in flour and 1 teaspoon salt. Cook 1 minute, stirring constantly. Gradually stir in 2 cups reserved broth and milk. Cook over medium heat about 3 to 5 minutes, stirring constantly, until mixture thickens. Remove from heat and gradually add half of mixture to beaten eggs in a small bowl. Mix well. Blend egg mixture slowly into the remaining hot mixture in the saucepan. Cook 3 to 4 minutes. Remove from heat. Preheat oven to 375F (190C). Butter a 2-1/2-quart casserole. Put HERBED STUFFING MIX in casserole. Pour half the sauce over stuffing. Add pieces of deboned chicken. Add remaining sauce. In a small bowl, mix bread crumbs with 1/4 cup melted butter or margarine and sprinkle over casserole. Bake 20 to 30 minutes, until bubbly. Makes 8 servings.

Scallop Casserole

A deep-sea delicacy.

1 cup chopped onion
1 tablespoon butter or
   margarine
1/2 cup water
1/2 teaspoon salt
1 lb. frozen scallops, thawed
4 eggs, slightly beaten
2 cups HERBED STUFFING
   MIX, page 17
4 slices Swiss cheese

In a medium saucepan, sauté onion in butter or margarine until tender. Add water and salt. Bring to a boil and add scallops. Cook 5 minutes over medium-high heat. Preheat oven to 350F (175C). Lightly butter a 2-quart casserole. Combine eggs and HERBED STUFFING MIX in casserole. Stir in scallop mixture. Bake 25 to 30 minutes. Remove from oven. Top with cheese slices. Return to oven just long enough to melt cheese. Makes 4 servings.

No-Fuss Swiss Steak Cubes

Put everything but the noodles in a Dutch oven and let it simmer 4 hours.

2 lbs. lean beef, cut in
   1-1/2-inch cubes
3 tablespoons all-purpose flour
1 (4-oz.) can diced or chopped
   green chilies
1 pkg. ONION SEASONING
   MIX, page 18
1/2 lb. fresh mushrooms or 1
   (8-oz.) can mushrooms,
   drained
1 (28-oz.) can tomatoes, crushed
2 cups water
3 cups hot cooked noodles,
   buttered

Dredge beef cubes in flour; place in Dutch oven. Add green chilies, ONION SEASONING MIX, mushrooms, tomatoes and water. Stir to blend. Cover; place in cold oven. Turn oven to 300F (150C). Bake 3 to 4 hours until tender. After 2 hours, add more water if needed to keep mixture moist. Serve over hot buttered noodles. Makes 6 to 8 servings.

Onion Pot Roast

Thicken the drippings with a cornstarch-water mixture to make a tasty gravy.

1/2 teaspoon salt
Pinch pepper
3 to 4 lbs. beef arm roast or 7
   blade pot roast
3 tablespoons all-purpose flour
3 tablespoons vegetable
   shortening
1 pkg. ONION SEASONING
   MIX, page 18
1 cup water
4 medium carrots, peeled,
   quartered
3 celery stalks, cut in sticks
3 medium potatoes, cut in half
1 bay leaf

Preheat oven to 325F (165C). Sprinkle salt and pepper over roast. Dredge in flour, turning to coat all sides. In a Dutch oven, melt shortening over medium heat. Add roast, turning to brown all sides. In a small bowl, combine ONION SEASONING MIX and water. Pour over roast. Add carrots, celery, potatoes and bay leaf; cover. Bake 3 hours until meat is tender. On a platter, arrange cooked vegetables around roast. Serve immediately. Makes 6 or 8 servings.

Variation
Foil-Wrapped Chuck Steak: Substitute 3 pounds chuck steak about 1 inch thick for roast. Omit flour and shortening. Reduce water to 1/2 cup. Place steak on an 18" x 12" rectangle of heavy-duty foil in a large baking pan. Sprinkle meat with ONION SEASONING MIX, salt and pepper. Carefully pour water over steak. Arrange carrots, celery and potatoes over steak. Dot with 2 tablespoons butter or margarine. Fold foil tightly against meat and vegetables. Bake 2 to 2-1/2 hours at 450F (230C). Serve as directed above. Makes 6 servings.

Apricot Chicken

Use pineapple tidbits and orange marmalade in place of apricot halves and apricot jam.

2 (3-lb.) frying chickens, cut up
1 (8-oz.) bottle Russian salad
    dressing
1 (16-oz.) can apricot halves,
    drained
1 cup apricot jam
1 pkg. ONION SEASONING
    MIX, page 18
Parsley sprigs, for garnish

Preheat oven to 350F (175C). Rinse chickens. Pat dry with paper towels; set aside. In a medium bowl, combine salad dressing, apricot halves, apricot jam and ONION SEASONING MIX. Place chicken pieces on 2 ungreased large baking sheets with raised sides. Pour sauce evenly over chicken pieces. Bake uncovered 1-1/4 hours in preheated oven until chicken is lightly browned. Arrange baked chicken on a large platter. Spoon drippings over chicken pieces. Garnish with parsley sprigs. Makes 8 servings.

Company Beef Brisket

Begin baking the brisket in the morning so it will be ready for your evening meal.

1 (5-lb.) beef brisket
1 pkg. ONION SEASONING
    MIX, page 18
2 tablespoons water
1 teaspoon salt
1/4 teaspoon pepper
3 tablespoons butter or
    margarine
10 small boiling onions, peeled
1/4 lb. small fresh mushrooms

Preheat oven to 350F (175C). Cut two 18" x 12" pieces of heavy-duty foil. Place 1 piece of foil on a large baking sheet with raised sides. Place brisket in center of foil. Sprinkle evenly with ONION SEASONING MIX, water, salt and pepper. Cut 1 tablespoon butter or margarine in pieces; dot evenly over meat. Bring 2 short ends of foil together over meat. Fold tight against meat; fold sides to make a tight seal. Repeat with second piece of foil, making a double covering of foil. Bake 1 hour in preheated oven. Reduce heat to 250F (120C). Bake 9 hours longer. In a medium sauce-pan, melt remaining 2 tablespoons butter or margarine. Add boiling onions. Sauté until tender when pierced with a fork. Add mushrooms; sauté 3 or 4 minutes longer. Unwrap meat. Pour drippings into onion mixture, stirring to combine. Slice meat, arranging slices on a platter. To serve, pour onion mixture over sliced brisket. Makes 18 to 20 servings.

Variation
To cook a 3- or 4-pound brisket, bake 30 minutes in pre-heated oven at 350F (175C), then 5 or 6 hours longer at 250F (120C).

Apricot Chicken

Company Chicken Roll-Ups

Your guests will rave about these tender chicken nuggets.

1/2 cup WHITE SAUCE MIX,
    page 22
1 cup cool water
1 cup shredded Cheddar cheese
    (4 oz.)
1 (4-oz.) can sliced mushrooms,
    drained
6 whole chicken breasts, skinned
    and boned
Flour
1 teaspoon salt
1 egg, slightly beaten
1 cup milk
2 cups dry bread crumbs
Vegetable oil for frying

In a small saucepan, combine WHITE SAUCE MIX with cool water. Cook over low heat until thick and smooth, stirring constantly. Add shredded Cheddar cheese and mushrooms. Stir until cheese is melted. Pour into an 8-inch square pan. Chill until set. Lay large pieces of chicken breasts on a generously floured surface with sides just touching. Fill in any gaps with small pieces of chicken. Sprinkle generously with flour. Cover with plastic wrap and pound together with a wooden mallet. Roll lightly with a rolling pin to form a rectangular shape, about 8" x 20". Remove plastic wrap. Sprinkle with salt. Cut cheese mixture in 1/2- to 3/4-inch strips. Lay about half of cheese strips along the long edge of chicken. Carefully wrap chicken around cheese mixture and roll up lengthwise like a jellyroll. With a sharp knife, cut into 2- to 3-inch pieces. Combine egg and milk in a shallow dish. Dip chicken pieces in egg mixture, then in bread crumbs. Place on a wire rack to dry out, about 15 minutes. Preheat oven to 350F (175C). Fry chicken in hot oil about 2 to 3 minutes on each side, until golden. Place in a 13" x 9" baking pan. Cover and bake 45 minutes, until chicken is tender. Melt remaining cheese mixture and serve over chicken rolls. Makes 8 to 10 servings.

Note
After chicken has been breaded, it can be loosely covered and refrigerated for a day, then cooked the next day. Breaded chicken rolls can also be frozen on a baking sheet, then stored in an airtight bag in freezer. Thaw several hours, then fry and bake as directed.

Rancher's Sloppy Joes

Feed a hungry crowd!

2 cups MEAT SAUCE MIX,
    page 24, thawed
1/4 cup brown sugar, firmly
    packed
2 tablespoons vinegar
1/2 cup ketchup
1 tablespoon mustard
6 hamburger buns

In a medium saucepan, combine MEAT SAUCE MIX, brown sugar, vinegar, ketchup and mustard. Cover and cook over medium heat about 10 minutes, until heated through. Serve over hamburger buns. Makes 6 servings.

Shrimp and Vegetable Stir-Fry

For a less expensive dish, substitute frozen cooked shrimp for the fresh shrimp.

About 1-1/4 lbs. broccoli
4 tablespoons vegetable oil
1 medium onion, thinly sliced
3/4 lb. fresh mushrooms, thinly
    sliced
2 tablespoons vegetable oil
3/4 lb. fresh shrimp, shelled,
    deveined
1-1/2 cups ORIENTAL
    STIR-FRY MIX, page 22
2 cups fresh bean sprouts
3 cups hot cooked rice

Cut broccoli stems into 1/4-inch pieces. Cut flowerets into 3/4-inch pieces; set aside. In a large skillet or wok, heat 4 tablespoons oil over medium heat. Add cut broccoli stems, sliced onion and sliced mushrooms. Cook and stir until stems are crisp-tender, 5 to 7 minutes. Add 2 tablespoons oil. When oil is hot, add shrimp and broccoli flowerets. Cook and stir 5 to 7 minutes longer. Spoon ORIENTAL STIR-FRY MIX over vegetables. Stir gently until mixture thickens slightly. Gently stir in bean sprouts; cook 1 minute longer. To serve, spoon hot mixture over cooked rice. Makes 4 to 6 servings.

Stir-Fry Cashew Chicken

Entertain your guests with this oriental dish.

3 chicken breast halves, skinned,
    boned
About 1/3 cup vegetable oil
1 lb. fresh green beans, cut in
    1-inch pieces
1 yam, cut in 1/4-inch slices
1 (8-oz.) can water chestnuts,
    drained, sliced
1-1/2 cups ORIENTAL
    STIR-FRY MIX, page 22
1 (3-oz.) pkg. cashew nuts
1 to 2 tablespoons water, if
    needed
3 cups hot cooked rice

Cut chicken into thin strips; set aside. In a large skillet or wok, heat 2 to 3 tablespoons oil. Add chicken. Stir constantly over medium heat until meat is tender, 4 to 5 minutes. Drain chicken on paper towels; cover and keep warm. Add 2 to 3 tablespoons of the remaining oil to skillet or wok. Add green beans. Cook and stir about 3 minutes. Add yam pieces. Cook and stir until beans are crisp-tender, 3 to 4 minutes. Add cooked chicken, water chestnuts and ORIENTAL STIR-FRY MIX. Cook and stir until sauce is slightly thickened, about 10 minutes. Stir in nuts and water, if needed to make a thinner sauce. Simmer 2 minutes longer. Serve over hot cooked rice. Makes 4 to 6 servings.

Teriyaki Beef and Vegetables

Have the meat and vegetables sliced and the rice cooked before you heat the oil.

1 lb. top sirloin
4 medium carrots
3 medium zucchini
About 1/3 cup vegetable oil
2 tablespoons brown sugar
1-1/2 cups ORIENTAL
   STIR-FRY MIX, page 22
3 cups hot cooked rice
4 green onions, thinly sliced, for
   garnish

On a cutting board, cut meat, carrots and zucchini in thin diagonal slices. Place 3 or 4 paper towels in a medium bowl; set aside. Heat 3 tablespoons oil in a large skillet or wok. Add meat slices; stir constantly over medium heat until meat is no longer red, 3 to 4 minutes. Use a slotted spoon to remove cooked meat to prepared bowl. Cover; keep warm. Add about 2 tablespoons of the remaining oil to skillet or wok. Add carrot slices. Cook and stir 2 to 3 minutes. Add zucchini slices. Cook and stir 2 to 3 minutes longer. Stir in cooked meat, brown sugar and ORIENTAL STIR-FRY MIX. Cook and stir until mixture thickens slightly. Serve over hot cooked rice. Garnish with sliced green onions. Makes 4 to 6 servings.

Tuna-Cheese Swirls

A treat for your eyes as well as your mouth.

1 (12-1/2-oz.) can light tuna,
   drained
1 cup frozen peas
1 (10-1/2-oz.) can chicken-rice
   soup
1-1/2 cups QUICK MIX, page 11
1/3 cup milk or water
3/4 cup shredded Cheddar
   cheese (3 oz.)

Preheat oven to 425F (220C). Butter a 1-1/2-quart casserole. Combine tuna, peas and chicken-rice soup in a medium bowl. Pour into prepared casserole. In a small bowl, combine QUICK MIX and milk or water. Stir until blended. On a lightly floured surface, knead dough gently 10 times. Roll out to 6" x 10" rectangle, about 1/4 inch thick. Sprinkle with cheese and roll like a jellyroll. Seal edge. Cut into 1/2-inch slices. Place slices on top of casserole. Bake 15 to 20 minutes, until biscuits are golden brown. Makes 4 to 6 servings.

Teriyaki Beef and Vegetables

Stuffed Hard Rolls

Let the kids help make these!

2 cups MEAT SAUCE MIX,
    page 24, thawed
1 cup shredded Cheddar cheese
    (4 oz.)
8 hard rolls, sliced

In a medium saucepan, simmer MEAT SAUCE MIX about 10 minutes until heated through. Remove from heat. Stir in shredded Cheddar cheese. Pull a small amount of bread from centers of hard rolls. Fill each roll with 1/4 cup of meat sauce-cheese mixture. Makes 8 stuffed rolls.

Stuffed Green Peppers

This colorful dish will satisfy your appetite.

2 cups MEAT SAUCE MIX,
    page 24, thawed
2 cups cooked rice, or 1 can
    whole kernel corn, drained
6 to 8 cups water
8 green peppers, seeds and
    membranes removed
1/2 cup shredded Cheddar
    cheese (2 oz.)

Preheat oven to 350F (175C). In a small saucepan, simmer MEAT SAUCE MIX and cooked rice about 10 minutes, until heated through. Bring water to a rapid boil in a large saucepan. Put green peppers into water a few at a time and boil about 10 minutes. Drain. Fill green peppers with warmed MEAT SAUCE MIX and rice. Top with grated cheese. Bake in a shallow pan 10 to 15 minutes. Makes 8 stuffed green peppers.

Hamburger Trio Skillet

Quick, easy and good.

2 cups MEAT SAUCE MIX,
    page 24, thawed
2 cups cooked rice
1 (17-oz.) can whole kernel corn
1/4 teaspoon thyme
1/2 cup chopped green pepper

Combine all ingredients in a medium skillet. Cover and cook over medium heat about 10 to 15 minutes, until heated through. Serve from skillet. Makes 4 to 6 servings.

Hamburger-Noodle Skillet

Excellent for a busy day.

2 cups MEAT SAUCE MIX,
   page 24, thawed
2 cups cooked noodles
2 cups cooked mixed vegetables,
   with liquid
1 (8-oz.) can seasoned tomato
   sauce
1/2 cup shredded Cheddar
   cheese (2 oz.)
1 teaspoon chopped parsley

In a medium skillet, combine MEAT SAUCE MIX, cooked noodles, cooked mixed vegetables and tomato sauce. Cover and cook over medium heat about 10 to 15 minutes, stirring occasionally, until heated through. Sprinkle shredded cheese and parsley on top. Do not stir. Cover and heat just long enough to melt cheese. Serve from skillet. Makes 4 to 6 servings.

Chili con Carne

Warms you from the inside out.

2 cups MEAT SAUCE MIX,
   page 24, thawed
2 (15-1/2-oz.) cans red kidney
   beans
1-1/2 teaspoons chili powder,
   more if desired

Combine ingredients in a medium saucepan. Cover and cook over medium heat about 15 minutes, until heated through. Makes 6 servings.

Sweet and Sour Meatballs

Not just plain meatballs!

1 tablespoon vegetable oil
1 (10-oz.) can pineapple chunks,
   drained, reserve juice
3 tablespoons cornstarch
1 tablespoon soy sauce
3 tablespoons vinegar
6 tablespoons water
1/2 cup brown sugar, firmly
   packed
1 container MEATBALL MIX,
   page 25, thawed
1 large green pepper, sliced
About 4 cups cooked rice

In a large skillet, combine oil and 1 cup drained pineapple juice, adding water if necessary to make 1 cup. In a small bowl, combine cornstarch, soy sauce, vinegar, water and brown sugar. Stir into juice mixture and cook over medium heat about 5 to 7 minutes until thick, stirring constantly. Add MEATBALL MIX, pineapple chunks and green pepper. Simmer 20 minutes until heated through. Serve over hot, cooked rice. Makes 6 servings.

Layered Casserole Complete

A hearty dinner for any family.

2 cups MEAT SAUCE MIX,
    page 24
1 (16-oz.) can French-cut green
    beans, drained, or 1 (10-oz.)
    pkg. frozen green beans
2 cups mashed potatoes
1 cup shredded Cheddar cheese
    (4 oz.)

Preheat oven to 350F (175C). Lightly butter a 1-1/2-quart casserole. Layer casserole with MEAT SAUCE MIX, green beans and mashed potatoes. Sprinkle grated cheese on top. Bake 25 to 30 minutes, until bubbly. Makes 4 servings.

Meatball Stew

Time for some good home cooking.

1/4 cup water
2 tablespoons all-purpose flour
1 beef bouillon cube
1 (1-lb.) can tomatoes
1 container MEATBALL MIX,
    page 25, thawed (about 30
    meatballs)
2 cups pared and sliced carrots
2 onions, quartered
1 cup sliced celery
1 cup peeled and cubed potatoes

In a medium saucepan, combine water, flour and bouillon. Stir until well-blended. Add tomatoes and cook about 5 minutes, until mixture thickens and boils, stirring constantly. Add MEATBALL MIX, carrots, onions, celery and potatoes. Cover and simmer 15 minutes. Preheat oven to 350F (175C). Pour into a 3-quart casserole. Cover and bake 1-1/2 hours. Makes 6 to 8 servings.

Green Chili Burros

That's Mexican!

3 cups MEXICAN MEAT MIX,
    page 27, thawed
6 large flour tortillas
Shredded lettuce, for garnish

Heat MEXICAN MEAT MIX in a small saucepan. Warm tortillas 1 at a time over low heat in a very large skillet until soft and pliable. Spread about 1/2 cup MEXICAN MEAT MIX over the lower 1/3 of each tortilla. Fold the bottom edge of each tortilla up over filling. Fold both sides toward the center and roll into a cylinder. Place on a heated plate, seam-side down, on a bed of shredded lettuce. Serve warm. Makes 6 burros.

Layered Casserole Complete

Chalupa

Top this with "hot" sauce for a really spicy meal.

1 lb. dry pinto beans
3 cups MEXICAN MEAT MIX,
    page 27, thawed
1 teaspoon salt
1 tablespoon chili powder
1 (10-oz.) bag corn chips
1 cup shredded longhorn or
    Monterey Jack cheese (4 oz.)
1/2 cup chopped onion
Shredded lettuce
2 tomatoes, chopped

Wash beans, put in a large pan and cover with water. Soak overnight. Cover and cook over low heat about 4 to 5 hours until beans are tender. Add water if needed. Add MEXICAN MEAT MIX, salt and chili powder. Cook uncovered about 1 hour, stirring occasionally, until heated through. Serve in small bowls over crisp corn chips. Garnish with cheese, onion, lettuce and tomatoes. Makes 8 servings.

Variation
Substitute 3 (15-oz.) cans pinto beans for dry pinto beans. Omit soaking and cooking until tender.

Chimichangas

These won the Southwest!

6 large flour tortillas
3 cups MEXICAN MEAT MIX,
    page 27, thawed
Vegetable oil for frying
Shredded lettuce
1 (7-oz.) can green chili salsa
2 tomatoes, chopped
1 cup Guacamole, see below
1 cup dairy sour cream
6 ripe olives, for garnish

Guacamole:
2 ripe avocados, pared and
    mashed
1 teaspoon lemon juice
Salt and pepper to taste
Few drops of hot pepper sauce

Warm tortillas in microwave about 30 seconds. Heat MEXICAN MEAT MIX in a small saucepan. Heat 1/2-inch deep oil to 400F (205C) in a large skillet. Spread about 1/2 cup MEXICAN MEAT MIX over the lower third of each tortilla. Fold the bottom edges of each tortilla up over filling. Fold both sides toward the center and roll into a cylinder. Secure rolled tortillas with a toothpick. Fry 2 chimichangas at a time in hot oil about 2 minutes until golden and crisp. Drain on paper towels. Serve hot over a layer of shredded lettuce. Top with green chili salsa, tomatoes, Guacamole and sour cream. Garnish each with an olive. Makes 6 chimichangas.

Guacamole
Combine all ingredients in a small bowl.

1. *Fold the bottom edge of each tortilla over the meat filling, and fold both sides toward the center.*

2. *Roll each tortilla into a cylinder. Secure with a toothpick.*

3. *Serve Chimichangas over lettuce, topped with green chili salsa, tomatoes, Guacamole and sour cream.*

Sour Cream Enchiladas

MEXICAN MEAT MIX wins again!

1 (10-oz.) can enchilada sauce
1 (16-oz.) can whole tomatoes,
    undrained and finely chopped
Vegetable oil for frying
12 corn tortillas
3 cups MEXICAN MEAT MIX,
    page 27, thawed
1-1/2 cups shredded Cheddar
    cheese (6 oz.)
1-1/2 cups dairy sour cream

Combine enchilada sauce and chopped tomatoes in a medium saucepan. Cook over medium heat until mixture boils. Reduce heat and simmer. Heat oil over medium-high heat in a small skillet. Dip one tortilla at a time in hot oil for several seconds, then dip in hot enchilada sauce mixture. Set aside. Heat MEXICAN MEAT MIX in a small saucepan. Place about 1/4 cup MEXICAN MEAT MIX on each tortilla and sprinkle with 2 tablespoons shredded Cheddar cheese. Roll up and place close together in a shallow casserole dish, seam-side down. Pour remaining sauce over enchiladas. Sprinkle with additional shredded cheese. Bake about 15 minutes, until bubbly. Spoon sour cream over enchiladas and serve hot. Makes about 6 servings.

Taco Supreme

For a super Mexican sandwich!

Vegetable oil for frying
3 cups MEXICAN MEAT MIX,
    page 27, thawed
12 to 15 corn tortillas
2 cups shredded Cheddar cheese
    (8 oz.)
Shredded lettuce
2 fresh tomatoes, chopped
1/4 cup chopped green onion
1 (7-oz.) can green chili salsa

Heat 2 inches of oil to 375F (190C) in a large skillet. Heat MEXICAN MEAT MIX in a medium saucepan. Fry tortillas in hot oil. Using tongs, fold tortillas in half, then immediately open to 45-degree angle. Fry about 1 minute, until crisp. Drain on paper towels. Place 2 tablespoons MEXICAN MEAT MIX in each cooked tortilla. Top with shredded cheese, lettuce, tomatoes, green onion and green chili salsa. Makes 12 to 15 tacos.

Variation
For added convenience, use prefried, formed corn tortillas instead of forming your own. Or use flour tortillas warmed in the microwave for a soft-shell taco.

Cathy's Meatball Sandwiches

This knife and fork sandwich is a big hit with teenagers.

4 cups ITALIAN-STYLE
   MEAT MIX, page 26, thawed
1 tablespoon butter or
   margarine
1 cup fresh mushrooms, thinly
   sliced
6 to 8 French rolls or onion
   rolls, split
1/4 cup grated Romano cheese

In a medium saucepan, bring ITALIAN-STYLE MEAT MIX to a boil, about 10 minutes. In a small skillet, melt butter or margarine. Add mushrooms; sauté until tender, about 2 minutes. Spoon meat mixture evenly on bottom portions of rolls. Spoon sautéed mushrooms evenly over meat mixture. Sprinkle evenly with cheese. Cover with tops of rolls. Makes 6 to 8 servings.

Eggplant Parmesan

Refrigerate the casserole overnight, then bake it about 45 minutes at 375F (190C).

Oil for frying
1 medium eggplant, unpeeled
2 eggs, slightly beaten
2 tablespoons cold water
1-1/2 cups fine bread crumbs
2-1/2 cups ITALIAN-STYLE
   MEAT MIX, page 26, thawed
1/2 cup grated Parmesan or
   Romano cheese
2 (6-oz.) pkgs. sliced mozzarella
   cheese

Pour oil for frying 1/2 inch deep in a large skillet. Heat to 375F (190C). At this temperature, a 1-inch cube of bread will turn golden-brown in 50 seconds. Cut eggplant into 15 slices about 1/4 inch thick; set aside. In a small shallow dish or pie plate, beat eggs and water to combine; set aside. Pour bread crumbs into another small shallow dish or pie plate. Dip eggplant into egg mixture, then into bread crumbs. Turning once, brown coated eggplant slices in hot oil until tender when pierced with a fork. Add more oil, if needed. Preheat oven to 375F (190C). Butter a 2-quart casserole dish. Arrange 5 eggplant slices over bottom of dish, overlapping if necessary. Top evenly with about 1/3 of the ITALIAN-STYLE MEAT MIX, 1/3 of the grated Parmesan or Romano cheese and 1/3 of the mozzarella cheese slices. Repeat, making 2 more layers. Bake uncovered 30 to 40 minutes until cheese melts and sauce bubbles. Makes 6 servings.

Spaghetti Royale

Surprise unexpected company with this 30-minute dinner fit for a queen.

4 cups ITALIAN-STYLE
    MEAT MIX, page 26, thawed
1 (12-oz.) pkg. spaghetti, cooked,
    drained
Grated Romano or Parmesan
    cheese

In a medium saucepan, simmer ITALIAN-STYLE MEAT MIX over low heat until hot, about 15 to 20 minutes. Pour cooked spaghetti onto a large platter. Spoon sauce over spaghetti. Sprinkle with cheese. Makes 6 to 8 servings.

Stuffed Manicotti Shells

For special company or your special family.

12 manicotti shells, cooked
Water, salted slightly
1 pint ricotta cheese
1 egg, beaten
1/4 cup grated Parmesan cheese
1 tablespoon parsley flakes
4 cups ITALIAN COOKING
    SAUCE MIX, page 25,
    thawed
Romano and Parmesan cheese,
    for garnish

Cook manicotti shells in boiling salted water according to package directions. In a medium bowl, combine ricotta cheese, egg, Parmesan cheese and parsley flakes. Blend well. Stuff into cooked manicotti shells. Preheat oven to 350F (175C). Place 1 cup of the ITALIAN COOKING SAUCE MIX in bottom of a 13" x 9" baking dish. Place stuffed manicotti shells on top of sauce. Pour remaining sauce over top of shells. Sprinkle with Romano and Parmesan cheese, for garnish. Cover with foil and bake 30 minutes, until heated through. Makes 6 servings.

Chicken Cacciatore

Viva la Italian!

Vegetable oil for frying
1/2 cup all-purpose flour
1 teaspoon salt
1/4 teaspoon pepper
1 (4-lb.) fryer chicken, cut up
4 cups ITALIAN COOKING
    SAUCE MIX, page 25,
    thawed

Heat oil in a large skillet. Combine flour, salt and pepper in a plastic bag. Add chicken pieces 2 at a time and shake to coat with mixture. Brown chicken in hot oil until golden brown. Preheat oven to 350F (175C). Put chicken in a 13" x 9" baking dish. Pour ITALIAN COOKING SAUCE MIX over chicken. Cover with foil. Bake about 1 hour, until chicken is tender. Makes 4 to 6 servings.

Veal Parmigiana

Your friends will love it.

6 thin veal cutlets
1 egg, slightly beaten
2 to 3 tablespoons milk
3/4 cup seasoned dry bread
   crumbs
3/4 cup grated Parmesan cheese
Butter or olive oil for frying
2 cups ITALIAN COOKING
   SAUCE MIX, page 25
1 (8-oz.) mozzarella cheese,
   sliced

Pound veal cutlets until thin. Combine egg and milk in a small bowl. In another small bowl, combine dry bread crumbs and grated Parmesan cheese. Dip veal into egg mixture, then into bread crumb mixture. Let veal stand at least 15 minutes before cooking. Heat butter or olive oil in a large skillet. Sauté veal cutlets in butter or oil about 2 minutes on each side until crisp. Preheat oven to 400F (205C). Put veal into a 13" x 9" baking pan. Pour ITALIAN COOKING SAUCE MIX over top. Place a slice of mozzarella cheese on each cutlet. Bake 10 to 15 minutes, until veal is golden brown and cheese is melted. Makes 4 to 6 servings.

Variation
Use veal cutlets that are already breaded and omit egg, milk, bread crumbs and grated Parmesan cheese.

Last-Minute Lasagna

The blend of flavors is superb.

6 cups ITALIAN COOKING
   SAUCE MIX, page 25,
   thawed
1 (8-oz.) pkg. lasagna noodles,
   cooked
1 lb. ricotta cheese
3 cups shredded mozzarella
   cheese (12 oz.)
1 cup grated Romano and
   Parmesan cheese (3 oz.)

Preheat oven to 350F (175C). Lightly butter a 13" x 9" baking pan. Spread 1/3 of ITALIAN COOKING SAUCE MIX in bottom of pan. Cover with 1/3 of lasagna noodles. Add 1/3 of ricotta cheese, thinned with water for easier spreading, if necessary. Add 1/3 of mozzarella cheese and 1/3 of Romano and Parmesan cheese. Repeat layers twice, topping with Romano and Parmesan cheese. Cover with foil. Bake 30 to 35 minutes, until heated through. Let stand 10 minutes before serving. Makes 8 to 10 servings.

Variation
Substitute 6 cups ITALIAN-STYLE MEAT MIX, page 26, for ITALIAN COOKING SAUCE MIX.

Pork Chow Mein

Fried rice is a nice accompaniment to this recipe.

2 cups CUBED PORK MIX,
    page 28, thawed
1-1/2 cups water
3 tablespoons soy sauce
4 tablespoons butter or
    margarine
4 to 5 celery stalks, sliced
    diagonally 1/4 inch thick
1 cup thinly sliced fresh
    mushrooms
1 (8-oz.) can water chestnuts,
    drained, thinly sliced
2 cups fresh bean sprouts
4 green onions, thinly sliced
1 (9-1/2-oz.) can chow mein
    noodles

In a large saucepan, combine CUBED PORK MIX, water and soy sauce. Simmer over low heat about 5 minutes. In a medium skillet, melt butter or margarine. Add celery; sauté until crisp-tender, about 10 minutes. Add fresh mushrooms and water chestnuts. Sauté 2 minutes, stirring occasionally. Stir into pork mixture. Stir occasionally over medium heat 5 minutes. Gently stir in bean sprouts and green onion slices. Simmer 1 minute longer. Serve over chow mein noodles. Makes about 6 servings.

Sweet and Sour Pork

Serve this tangy sweet and sour sauce over rice, noodles or spaghetti squash.

1 (20-oz.) can pineapple chunks
2 cups CUBED PORK MIX,
    page 28, thawed
2 tablespoons white vinegar
1 tablespoon soy sauce
1/3 cup brown sugar, firmly
    packed
1/4 cup ketchup
1 medium green pepper, cut in
    julienne strips
3 cups hot cooked rice

Drain juice from pineapple into a large saucepan. Stir in CUBED PORK MIX, vinegar, soy sauce, brown sugar and ketchup. Stir occasionally over medium heat about 10 minutes. Stir in drained pineapple chunks and green pepper strips. Simmer about 2 minutes until heated through. Serve over hot cooked rice. Makes 4 to 6 servings.

Company Casserole

Introduce variety by using mostaccioli, rotini spirals or wheels rather than flat noodles.

2 cups ALL-PURPOSE
   GROUND BEEF MIX, page
   29, thawed
1 tablespoon sugar
1/2 teaspoon garlic salt
2 (8-oz.) cans tomato sauce
2 to 3 tablespoons water, if
   needed
1 (3-oz.) pkg. cream cheese,
   softened
1/4 to 1/2 cup milk
1 cup dairy sour cream
6 green onions, finely sliced
1 (8-oz.) pkg. noodles, cooked,
   drained
2 cups shredded Cheddar cheese
   (8 oz.)

Preheat oven to 350F (175C). Lightly butter a 2-quart casserole dish; set aside. In a medium saucepan, combine ALL-PURPOSE GROUND BEEF MIX, sugar, garlic salt and tomato sauce. Simmer over medium heat about 10 minutes. Add water if needed to keep mixture moist. In a small bowl, combine cream cheese, 1/4 cup milk and sour cream, stirring until smooth. Stir in additional milk if needed to make a medium-thick sauce. Stir in green onions. In prepared casserole dish, layer 1/2 of the cooked noodles, 1/4 of the meat mixture and 1/2 of the sour cream mixture. Repeat layers. Top evenly with shredded cheese. Bake 30 minutes in preheated oven until layers are heated through and cheese melts. Makes 6 to 8 servings.

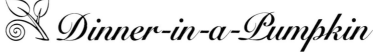

Dinner-in-a-Pumpkin

For a Halloween treat, paint a face on the pumpkin with acrylic paints before it is baked.

1 medium pumpkin
4 cups ALL-PURPOSE
   GROUND BEEF MIX, page
   29, thawed
1/4 cup soy sauce
2 tablespoons brown sugar,
   firmly packed
1 (4-oz.) can sliced mushrooms,
   drained
1 (10-1/2-oz.) can cream of
   chicken soup
2 cups hot cooked rice

Preheat oven to 375F (190C). Lightly grease a 10-inch circle in center of a baking sheet; set aside. Place pumpkin on a firm surface. Using a sharp knife, cut out stem end and about 3 inches around stem. Cut on a diagonal by slanting knife from outer edge of pumpkin toward center. Reserve top of pumpkin. Remove seeds and pulp; discard. In a medium bowl, combine ALL-PURPOSE GROUND BEEF MIX, soy sauce, brown sugar, mushrooms, soup and rice. Spoon mixture into pumpkin. Replace top of pumpkin. Place filled pumpkin on greased center of baking sheet. Bake about 1 hour in preheated oven until pumpkin is tender. To serve, spoon some of cooked pumpkin and meat filling onto plates. Makes 6 to 8 servings.

Saturday Stroganoff

Stroganoff lovers will love the convenience of this dish.

2 cups ALL-PURPOSE
   GROUND BEEF MIX, page
   29, thawed
1 (10-3/4-oz.) can cream of
   celery soup
1 (10-3/4-oz.) can cream of
   mushroom soup
3/4 cup milk
2 cups dairy sour cream
Cooked noodles
Poppy seeds, for garnish

In a large saucepan, combine ALL-PURPOSE GROUND BEEF MIX, cream of celery soup, cream of mushroom soup and milk. Stir until well-blended. Simmer about 10 minutes. Just before serving, add sour cream. Simmer 2 minutes. Serve over cooked noodles garnished with poppy seeds. Makes 4 to 6 servings.

Enchilada Casserole

A simple introduction to Mexican cookery.

1 (6-oz.) pkg. corn chips
2 cups ALL-PURPOSE
   GROUND BEEF MIX, page
   29, thawed
1 (15-oz.) can chili with beans
1 (10-oz.) can enchilada sauce
1 (8-oz.) can tomato sauce
1 cup dairy sour cream
1/2 cup shredded Cheddar
   cheese (2 oz.)

Preheat oven to 375F (190C). Lightly butter a 2-quart casserole. Crush 1/2 cup of the corn chips and reserve for top. In a medium bowl, combine remaining corn chips, ALL-PURPOSE GROUND BEEF MIX, chili, enchilada sauce and tomato sauce. Pour into prepared casserole. Bake about 20 minutes, until heated through. Remove from heat. Spread sour cream on top. Sprinkle with shredded cheese and reserved crushed corn chips. Bake 5 more minutes until cheese is melted. Makes 6 servings.

Hurry-Up Curry

Curry is a blend of spices, mild to quite hot in flavor.

2 cups ALL-PURPOSE
   GROUND BEEF MIX, page
   29, or 2 cups CUBED PORK
   MIX, page 28, thawed
1/3 cup ketchup
3/4 cup water
1 cup sliced fresh mushrooms
1 teaspoon curry powder
2 teaspoons steak sauce
2 teaspoons Worcestershire sauce
3/4 cup chutney, if desired
3 cups hot cooked rice

In a large skillet, combine ALL-PURPOSE GROUND BEEF MIX or CUBED PORK MIX, ketchup, water, mushrooms, curry powder, steak sauce and Worcestershire sauce. Stirring occasionally, cook over medium heat until heated through, about 10 minutes. If desired, spoon chutney into a small bowl. Serve curry mixture over hot cooked rice. Makes about 6 servings.

Mexican Delight

This Southwest combination will be a favorite at your next buffet dinner.

1 (30-oz.) can refried beans
2 cups ALL-PURPOSE
    GROUND BEEF MIX, page
    29, thawed
1 (4-oz.) can diced or chopped
    green chilies
3 cups shredded Monterey Jack
    cheese (12 oz.)
1 (7-oz.) can green chili salsa
1 large ripe avocado, peeled,
    pitted, mashed, or 1
    (7-3/4-oz.) pkg. frozen
    avocado dip, thawed
1 cup dairy sour cream
1 cup pitted ripe olives, for
    garnish
1 (10-oz.) pkg. corn chips

Preheat oven to 400F (205C). Lightly butter a 13" x 9" baking dish. Spread refried beans in bottom of dish. Spread ALL-PURPOSE GROUND BEEF MIX evenly over beans. Sprinkle chilies evenly over meat mixture. Sprinkle with shredded cheese. Drizzle green chili salsa over cheese. Bake about 30 minutes in preheated oven until hot and bubbly. Remove from oven. Spoon mashed avocado or avocado dip in center of casserole. Spoon sour cream in a circle around avocado. Arrange olives on sour cream and avocado. Tuck about 1/3 of the corn chips around edge of dish with points up. Serve with remaining corn chips. Makes 6 servings.

Oriental-Style Hamburger Skillet

If you prefer a crunchier texture, serve this mixture over Chinese-style noodles.

2 cups ALL-PURPOSE
    GROUND BEEF MIX, page
    29, thawed
3-1/2 cups water
2-1/4 cups instant rice
1/4 cup soy sauce
Salt to taste

In a large skillet, combine ALL-PURPOSE GROUND BEEF MIX, water, rice and soy sauce. Stirring occasionally, cook over medium heat until water is absorbed and rice is tender, about 10 minutes. Stir in salt to taste. Makes 4 to 6 servings.

Quick Chow Mein

For an even quicker meal, use canned chow mein vegetables.

1 (4-oz.) can mushroom pieces,
  drained
1 teaspoon ground ginger
2 tablespoons soy sauce
2 cups beef broth
2 cups CUBED PORK MIX,
  page 28 or 2 cups
  ALL-PURPOSE GROUND
  BEEF MIX, page 29, thawed
2 cups shredded Chinese
  cabbage
2 cups chopped celery
1/2 lb. fresh bean sprouts
1 (8-oz.) can water chestnuts,
  drained, sliced
2 tablespoons cornstarch
1/4 cup cold water
3 cups hot cooked rice
3 tablespoons snipped fresh
  parsley, for garnish
2 tablespoons sliced blanched
  almonds, for garnish

In a large skillet or wok, combine mushrooms, ginger, soy sauce and beef broth. Cover and simmer over medium heat 5 minutes. Add CUBED PORK MIX or ALL-PURPOSE GROUND BEEF MIX, cabbage, celery, bean sprouts and water chestnuts. Simmer until vegetables are hot, about 5 minutes. Stir cornstarch into cold water to dissolve. Stir into meat mixture. Continue stirring until mixture boils. Cover; simmer over low heat 5 minutes longer. Serve over hot cooked rice. Garnish with snipped parsley and sliced almonds. Makes 6 to 8 servings.

1. Add mix and vegetables to broth mixture. Simmer until vegetables are crisp-tender.

2. Serve over hot rice. Garnish with snipped parsley and sliced almonds.

 *Slumgullion*

Serve this quick combination on a day when time is short.

2 cups ALL-PURPOSE
   GROUND BEEF MIX, page
   29, thawed
1 (12-oz.) can whole-kernel corn
2 (8-oz.) cans tomato sauce
1 (6-oz.) pkg. noodles, cooked,
   drained

In a medium skillet, combine ALL-PURPOSE GROUND BEEF MIX, corn and tomato sauce. Stirring occasionally, simmer over medium heat about 15 minutes. Stir hot cooked noodles into meat mixture. Simmer 10 minutes. Makes 6 servings.

Variation
Stir 2 tablespoons butter or margarine and 1/2 teaspoon dried parsley leaves into hot cooked noodles. To serve, spoon noodles onto 6 plates. Spoon meat mixture over noodles.

 *Spaghetti Casserole*

Spaghetti for a crowd!

1 (12-oz.) pkg. spaghetti
Water, lightly salted
1 tablespoon sugar
3 cups shredded Cheddar cheese
   (12 oz.)
2 cups ALL-PURPOSE
   GROUND BEEF MIX, page
   29, thawed
1 (2-1/4-oz.) can mushrooms
1 (10-1/2-oz.) can tomato soup
1/2 cup milk
1 (15-oz.) jar spaghetti sauce

Preheat oven to 350F (175C). Butter a 2-1/2- to 3-quart casserole. Cook spaghetti in lightly salted water according to package directions. Put half of cooked spaghetti in bottom of prepared casserole. Sprinkle with half the sugar. Sprinkle half the grated cheese on top, then half the ALL-PURPOSE GROUND BEEF MIX, then half the mushrooms. Repeat layers. In a small bowl, combine tomato soup, milk and spaghetti sauce. Pour over entire casserole. If necessary, add more milk during baking to keep casserole moist. Bake 1 hour, until bubbly. Makes 6 to 8 servings.

 *Chicken Burgers*

Perfect for a Saturday afternoon lunch.

2 cups CHICKEN MIX page 30,
   thawed
1 cup barbecue sauce
8 hamburger buns

Combine CHICKEN MIX and barbecue sauce in a medium saucepan. Cook over medium heat about 10 minutes, until heated through. Serve over hamburger buns. Makes 8 burgers.

Hawaiian Haystack

When it's time for a Polynesian buffet, put the ingredients in order and let your guests stack 'em up!

2 (10-3/4-oz.) cans cream of
   chicken soup
1 cup chicken broth, page 30,
   thawed
2 cups CHICKEN MIX, page 30,
   thawed
4 cups cooked long-grain rice
1 (9-1/2-oz.) can chow mein
   noodles
3 medium tomatoes, sliced
1 cup chopped celery
1/2 cup chopped green pepper
1/2 cup chopped green onion
1 (20-oz.) can pineapple chunks,
   drained
1 cup shredded Cheddar cheese
   (4 oz.)
1/2 cup slivered almonds
1/2 cup coconut
1 (2-oz.) jar pimiento, drained
   and diced, if desired

Combine soup and chicken broth in a medium saucepan to make gravy. Stir to blend. Add CHICKEN MIX. Simmer about 8 to 10 minutes, until heated through. On 8 individual serving plates layer all ingredients. First stack rice, chow mein noodles, and chicken and gravy. Add tomatoes, celery, green pepper and green onion. Top this with pineapple chunks, shredded Cheddar cheese, and more chicken and gravy, if desired. Stack almonds, coconut and pimiento on top. Makes 8 servings.

Sweet and Sour Chicken

It's time for a Hawaiian delight!

1/2 cup water
5 tablespoons cornstarch
3/4 cup brown sugar, firmly
   packed
1 teaspoon salt
1 (20-oz.) can pineapple chunks,
   drained, reserving juice
2 cups CHICKEN MIX, page 30,
   thawed
2 tablespoons soy sauce
1/4 cup white vinegar
2 cups chicken broth, page 30,
   thawed
2 cups water
2 cups uncooked long-grain rice
1/2 cup thinly sliced onion
3/4 cup thinly sliced green
   peppers
2 large tomatoes, cut in wedges

In a small bowl, combine 1/2 cup water, cornstarch, brown sugar and salt. Stir until mixture is smooth. Combine reserved pineapple juice and brown sugar mixture in a large saucepan. Cook over medium heat about 5 to 7 minutes, until mixture starts to thicken. Add CHICKEN MIX, soy sauce and vinegar. Cover and simmer 15 minutes, stirring occasionally. Put chicken broth and 2 cups water in a large saucepan. Add rice. Cover and cook about 25 minutes. Add pineapple chunks, onion slices and green peppers to CHICKEN MIX mixture. Cook until vegetables are slightly tender. Just before serving, stir in tomato wedges. Serve over the hot, cooked rice. Makes 8 to 10 servings.

Hawaiian Haystack

Chicken Continental

CHICKEN MIX makes it easier.

1 (10-3/4-oz.) can cream of
    chicken soup
2 tablespoons grated onion
1 teaspoon salt
Dash of pepper
1 tablespoon parsley flakes
1/4 teaspoon thyme
2 cups chicken broth, page 30,
    thawed
2 cups CHICKEN MIX, page 30,
    thawed
2 cups instant rice

Preheat oven to 375F (190C). Lightly butter a 2-quart casserole. In a medium bowl, combine cream of chicken soup, onion, salt, pepper, parsley flakes, thyme and chicken broth. Stir until well-blended. Add CHICKEN MIX and instant rice. Put in prepared casserole. Cover and bake about 30 minutes, until rice is tender. Makes 6 servings.

Club Chicken Casserole

Keep this recipe up front!

2 cups chicken broth, page 30,
    thawed
1 cup uncooked long-grain rice
3 tablespoons butter or
    margarine
3 tablespoons all-purpose flour
1-1/2 teaspoons salt
1-2/3 cups evaporated milk
2 cups CHICKEN MIX, page 30,
    thawed
1 (10-oz.) pkg. frozen chopped
    broccoli, cooked and drained
1 (3-oz.) can sliced mushrooms,
    drained
1/4 cup toasted slivered almonds
Paprika, for garnish

Preheat oven to 350F (175C). Lightly butter an 11" x 7" baking pan. Combine chicken broth and rice in a large saucepan. Cook about 25 minutes, until rice is tender. Melt butter or margarine in a large saucepan. Gradually stir in flour and salt. Gradually add evaporated milk. Cook over medium heat about 5 minutes, stirring constantly, until mixture thickens and boils. Add CHICKEN MIX, cooked rice mixture, broccoli and mushrooms. Put in prepared baking pan. Top with toasted almonds and paprika. Bake 30 to 35 minutes, until bubbly. Makes 8 servings.

Variation
Substitute 1 (10-oz.) pkg. frozen peas for broccoli.

Creamy Chicken Enchiladas

If you prefer not to have to heat up the oil to soften the tortillas, you can quickly dip them in hot water instead.

2 cups CHICKEN MIX, page 30,
    thawed
1 (4-oz.) can diced green chilies
1 (7-oz.) can green chili salsa
2-1/2 cups shredded Jack cheese
    (10 oz.)
Vegetable oil for frying
8 (6-inch) flour tortillas
1 pint whipping cream (2 cups)
1/2 teaspoon salt
Sprinkle of paprika, for garnish
Chopped green onions, for
    garnish

In a medium bowl, combine CHICKEN MIX, green chilies, green chili salsa and 1 cup of the cheese. Heat oil over medium-high heat in medium skillet. Quickly dip tortillas in hot oil with tongs, one at a time, just to soften tortilla. Drain on paper towel. Preheat oven to 350F (175C). Put approximately 1/3 cup filling mixture in center of each tortilla and roll up. Place close together in a shallow casserole dish or baking pan, seam-side down. In medium bowl, combine whipping cream and salt. Pour cream mixture over pan of enchiladas and sprinkle with remaining cheese. Cover with foil. Bake 20 to 25 minutes until bubbly. Garnish with paprika and green onions. Makes 4 to 6 servings.

Mexican Chicken Bake

You'll need corn tortillas for this one.

1 (10-3/4-oz.) can cream of
    mushroom soup
1 (10-3/4-oz.) can cream of
    chicken soup
2-3/4 cups milk
2 cups CHICKEN MIX, page 30,
    thawed
1/2 teaspoon salt
1 large onion, finely chopped
1 (7-oz.) can green chili salsa
2-1/2 cups shredded Cheddar
    cheese (10 oz.)
12 corn tortillas, each cut into 8
    pieces

Preheat oven to 350F (175C). Lightly butter a 2-quart casserole. In a medium bowl, combine cream of mushroom soup, cream of chicken soup and milk. Stir to blend well. Add CHICKEN MIX, salt, onion, green chili salsa and 2 cups of the shredded cheese. Layer tortilla pieces and chicken mixture alternately in prepared casserole, topping with chicken mixture. Top with remaining shredded cheese. Bake 35 to 45 minutes, until bubbly. Makes 8 servings.

Variation
For a "hotter" flavor, substitute 1 (4-oz.) can diced green chilies for green chili salsa.

Chicken à la King

A dish truly fit for a king!

1/2 cup butter or margarine
1 cup chopped celery
1 (4-oz.) can mushrooms or 1/4
  lb. fresh mushrooms
1/2 cup all-purpose flour
2 cups chicken broth, page 30,
  thawed
2 cups CHICKEN MIX, page 30,
  thawed
1 cup milk
1/4 cup chopped pimiento, if
  desired
1 tablespoon parsley flakes
Cooked rice
Slivered almonds, for garnish

Melt butter or margarine in a large skillet. Add celery and mushrooms. Sauté until tender. Blend in flour and let simmer 1 minute. Slowly add chicken broth. Cook about 3 to 5 minutes, stirring constantly until thick. Add CHICKEN MIX, milk, pimiento, if desired, and parsley flakes. Simmer 10 minutes. Serve over hot, cooked rice. Garnish with slivered almonds. Makes 6 servings.

Variation
For a party luncheon, serve in baked puff pastry shells.

1. Melt margarine or butter in a skillet, then add chopped celery and sliced mushrooms. Sauté until tender.

2. Simmer the ingredients in chicken broth 10 minutes. Serve in baked puff pastry shells for a luncheon or over hot cooked rice for dinner.

Chicken-Cashew Casserole

A catchy combination of cashew nuts and chow mein noodles.

2 (10-3/4-oz.) cans cream of
    mushroom soup
1-1/4 cups chicken broth, page
    30, thawed, or water
1/2 cup chopped onion
2 cups chopped celery
2 cups CHICKEN MIX, page 30,
    thawed
1 (9-1/2-oz.) can chow mein
    noodles
1 cup cashew nuts

Preheat oven to 350F (175C). Lightly butter a 2-quart casserole. In a medium bowl, combine cream of mushroom soup, chicken broth or water, onion and celery. Stir to blend. Add CHICKEN MIX, chow mein noodles and cashew nuts. Pour into prepared casserole. Bake, uncovered, 45 minutes. Makes 6 to 8 servings.

Deep-Dish Pot Pie

To bake the pie immediately, follow the instructions for baking given below.

1 pkg. FIVE-WAY BEEF MIX
    with hamburger, page 31,
    thawed
Single Freezer Pie Crust,
    unbaked, page 33
1 egg
1 tablespoon vegetable oil

Turn FIVE-WAY BEEF MIX into an 8- or 9-inch square baking dish or a 2-1/2-quart casserole dish. Roll out pastry to a 10-inch square or to fit casserole dish. Place pastry over dish. Trim, letting dough extend 1/2-inch beyond edge of dish. Fold under edge; flute. To freeze unbaked pie: Wrap airtight in heavy-duty freezer wrap or heavy-duty foil. Store in freezer. Use within 6 months. To bake frozen pie: Preheat oven to 425F (220C). Cut slits in crust to let steam escape. In a small bowl, beat egg and oil with a fork or a wire whisk. Brush evenly on crust with a pastry brush, covering entire crust. Bake 45 to 60 minutes in preheated oven until deep golden brown. Makes 4 to 6 servings.

Vegetable and Cheese Casserole

Serve this colorful casserole with hot biscuits, page 132.

3 tablespoons butter or
    margarine
1 cup dry bread crumbs
1 pkg. FIVE-WAY BEEF MIX
    made with hamburger, page
    31, thawed
1 cup shredded Cheddar cheese
    or Monterey Jack cheese (4
    oz.)
1 (10-1/2-oz.) can cream of
    celery soup

Preheat oven to 350F (175C). In a small skillet, melt butter or margarine over medium-low heat. Stir in bread crumbs. Cook and stir until crumbs are crisp and golden brown. Butter a 2-1/2-quart casserole dish. Add FIVE-WAY BEEF MIX, cheese and soup. Stir gently to combine. Top casserole with browned crumbs. Bake 30 minutes. Makes 4 to 6 servings.

Meat and Potato Pie

Serve this family favorite with ketchup or chili sauce.

Double Freezer Pie Crust,
    unbaked, page 33
1 lb. lean ground beef
1/2 cup milk
1 pkg. ONION SEASONING
    MIX, page 18
1/8 teaspoon pepper
1 (12-oz.) pkg. hash brown
    potatoes, thawed, or 4 cups
    grated cooked potatoes

Prepare bottom crust in a 9-inch pie plate; set aside. Preheat oven to 350F (175C). In a medium bowl, combine ground beef, milk, ONION SEASONING MIX and pepper. Press into pastry lined pie plate. Top with potatoes. Cover with top crust. Trim and flute edges. Cut slits in top crust to let steam escape. Bake 1 hour until crust is golden brown. Makes 6 servings.

Spanish Cheese Pie

You can tell if the filling is set by shaking the pie with gentle back and forth motions.

Single Freezer Pie Crust,
  unbaked, page 33
1-1/2 cups shredded Monterey
  Jack cheese (6 oz.)
1 (4 oz.) can diced or chopped
  green chilies
1 cup shredded Cheddar cheese
  (4 oz.)
4 eggs
1-1/2 cups half-and-half
1/4 teaspoon salt
1/8 teaspoon ground cumin

Prepare pie crust in a 9-inch pie plate; set aside. Preheat oven to 350F (175C). Sprinkle Monterey Jack cheese in bottom of unbaked pie crust. Top evenly with green chilies and 1/2 cup Cheddar cheese. In a medium bowl, beat eggs thoroughly. Stir in half-and-half, salt and cumin. Pour over cheese in pie crust. Top with remaining 1/2 cup Cheddar cheese. Bake 40 to 60 minutes until set. Makes 4 to 6 servings.

Turkey Dinner Pie

Simple, but special!

Double Freezer Pie Crust,
  unbaked, page 33
2-1/2 cups cooked turkey or
  chicken, cut in 1/2-inch cubes
2 cups leftover turkey gravy
1 (10-oz.) pkg. frozen carrots
  and peas, thawed
1 (8-oz.) can onions, halved
1 teaspoon salt
1/8 teaspoon pepper
1/8 teaspoon ground thyme

Prepare bottom crust in a 9-inch pie plate. Preheat oven to 425F (220C). In a large bowl, combine turkey or chicken, gravy, carrots and peas, onions, salt, pepper and thyme. Stir to distribute evenly. Pour into pastry shell. Cover with top crust. Trim and flute edges. Cut slits in top crust to let steam escape. Bake 35 to 40 minutes in preheated oven until golden brown. Makes 6 servings.

Breakfast and Brunch

The aroma of freshly baked muffins coming from your kitchen is the best way to wake up your family. Is it too hard for you to get things baking soon enough to do that? With Master Mixes on your pantry shelf, you have a whole collection of Breakfast and Brunch delights to serve your family or guests in minutes. You already know that a well-balanced breakfast contributes to your family's well-being throughout the day. A mix you've made is a great way to begin those easy, nutritious meals.

The Orange Butterflake Rolls are beautiful rolls that look fancy but are easy to make with HOT ROLL MIX. Serve this treat with a favorite beverage and fruit.

Look closely at the rolls and breads in this chapter and Breads and Rolls, page 124. By making the basic dough from HOT ROLL MIX, you can finish a variety of baked goods, such as Cinnamon Rolls, Cream Cheese Swirls and Swedish Cinnamon Twists.

Favorite Wheat Pancakes is a great choice for breakfast. Serve these light tender pancakes with a variety of toppings. You won't believe how wonderful they taste. Puff Oven Pancakes create a brunch spectacular right before your eyes. Try them for a late evening supper, too. For best results, we suggest you let pancake batters stand about 5 minutes before cooking.

Serve Molasses-Bran Muffins with a cold glass of milk for a complete breakfast you can eat in a hurry. You'll feel healthy, too. Or maybe Apple Muffins or Blueberry Muffins appeal to you more.

For weekends with company, the Sausage-Cheese Breakfast Strata is wonderfully different. It is quickly prepared the night before and just popped in the oven to bake in the morning. Let mixes help you entertain with ease.

Tip for Muffin Section

Freeze Ahead Muffins: Line muffin cup with paper liner, fill with muffin batter. Pop the pan in the freezer. When frozen hard, remove from pan and transfer to freezer container. (Note baking time and temperature on container.) When ready to bake, place frozen muffins back into pan and place in preheated oven. Increase baking time 3 to 6 minutes.

Tip for Breakfast and Brunch Section

Prepare extra waffles or French toast. Place on baking sheets in a single layer; cover. Freeze until solid. When frozen remove from baking sheets and store in plastic freezer bags or container. When ready to serve, thaw in microwave or at room temperature for a few minutes then pop in toaster to crisp.

Sunshine Coffee Cake

A moist muffin-textured cake—with a variety of toppings.

3 cups QUICK MIX, page 11
1/3 cup sugar
1 egg, slightly beaten
1 cup milk or water
1 teaspoon vanilla extract
Cinnamon Crumble Topping,
    see below

Cinnamon Crumble Topping:
1/3 cup all-purpose flour
1/2 cup dry bread crumbs or
    cookie or cake crumbs
1/2 cup brown sugar, firmly
    packed
1 teaspoon ground cinnamon
1/4 cup butter or margarine

Preheat oven to 350F (175C). Butter an 8-inch square pan. In a medium bowl, combine QUICK MIX and sugar until evenly distributed. In a small bowl, combine egg, milk or water and vanilla. Stir until just blended. Add liquid ingredients all at once to the dry ingredients. Fold mixture together until blended. Prepare Cinnamon Crumble Topping. Spread half the batter in the prepared pan. Spread half of topping over the batter. Top with remaining batter and topping. Bake 40 to 50 minutes. Makes one 8-inch cake.

Cinnamon Crumble Topping

In a medium bowl combine flour, crumbs, brown sugar and cinnamon. With a pastry blender, cut in butter or margarine until mixture is crumbly.

Variations

Fruit Crumble Topping: Prepare 1-1/2 cups sweetened, sliced, fresh or frozen fruit. Spread over first half of batter and top with Cinnamon Crumble Topping, see above. Proceed according to recipe directions.

Apple Crumble Topping: Add 1-1/2 cups peeled, finely chopped apples and 1/2 cup raisins to Cinnamon Crumble Topping, see above. Spread mixture on top of coffeecake before baking for a crusty topping, or on bottom of pan for a moist coffeecake.

Date-Nut Topping: Omit Cinnamon Crumble Topping. In a small bowl, combine 1 cup brown sugar and 1/4 cup all-purpose flour until well-blended. In another bowl, mix together 1/2 cup chopped, pitted dates and 1 teaspoon vanilla; add to brown sugar mixture. Stir in 1/2 cup chopped nuts. Cut in 1/4 cup butter or margarine until mixture is crumbly. Proceed according to recipe directions.

Chocolate Swirl Topping: Omit Cinnamon Crumble Topping. Melt 1/3 cup semisweet chocolate chips in a small saucepan. In a small bowl, combine 1/3 cup flaked coconut, 1/4 cup chopped nuts, 1/4 cup sugar and 1 tablespoon melted butter or margarine. Pour coffeecake batter into prepared pan. Spoon melted chocolate over batter. With a knife, cut through batter several times for a marbled effect. Sprinkle coconut mixture evenly over the top, and bake as directed above.

Swedish Cinnamon Twists

A mouth watering experience!

1 tablespoon active dry yeast
1 tablespoon sugar
1/4 cup warm water
1 cup buttermilk
1/4 teaspoon baking soda
1/2 cup butter or margarine,
　melted
2 eggs, beaten
4 to 5 cups HOT ROLL MIX,
　page 12
Cinnamon Filling, see below
3 tablespoons butter or
　margarine, melted
Powdered Sugar Glaze, see
　below

Cinnamon Filling:
1/2 cup brown sugar, firmly
　packed
1/2 teaspoon ground cinnamon
1/2 cup chopped nuts

Powdered Sugar Glaze:
1-1/2 cups sifted powdered
　sugar
1/2 tablespoon butter or
　margarine, melted
2 tablespoons hot water

In a small bowl, dissolve yeast and sugar in warm water. Set aside. Bring buttermilk to a boil in a small saucepan; buttermilk should curdle. In a large bowl, combine buttermilk, baking soda and 1/2 cup melted butter or margarine. Add eggs. When mixture is lukewarm, add dissolved yeast mixture. Gradually stir in 4 cups HOT ROLL MIX until the soft dough forms a ball. On a lightly floured surface, knead dough about 5 minutes until smooth and elastic. Add additional HOT ROLL MIX if necessary to make a soft, but not too sticky dough. Lightly butter bowl. Put dough in bowl and turn to butter top. Cover dough with a damp towel and let rise in a warm place until doubled in bulk, about 1 hour. Generously grease 2 baking sheets. Prepare Cinnamon Filling. Punch down dough. Roll out to a 12" x 10" rectangle. Brush dough with 3 tablespoons melted butter or margarine. Sprinkle Cinnamon Filling lengthwise over half of dough to within 1/2 inch of long edge. Fold rectangle in half lengthwise to cover filling. Seal dough edges with the edge of a plate. With a pizza cutter, cut dough into 24 strips, about 3/4 inch wide. Twist each strip twice and place strips 1 inch apart on prepared baking sheets. Cover and let rise until doubled in bulk, about 30 to 40 minutes. Preheat oven to 375F (190C). Bake 10 to 12 minutes, until golden brown. Prepare Powdered Sugar Glaze, and brush on while rolls are still warm. Makes about 24 twists.

Cinnamon Filling
Combine brown sugar, cinnamon and nuts in a small bowl.

Powdered Sugar Glaze
Combine powdered sugar, melted butter or margarine and hot water in a small bowl to make a thin glaze.

Aebleskivers

Aebleskivers are usually served with apple slices, apple butter or applesauce.

2 eggs, separated
1-1/2 cups BUTTERMILK
   PANCAKE AND WAFFLE
   MIX, page 13
1 cup water
2 tablespoons melted butter
Butter for frying
Powdered sugar, for garnish, if
   desired

In a medium bowl, beat egg yolks until pale. Stir in BUT-TERMILK PANCAKE AND WAFFLE MIX, water and 2 tablespoons melted butter until blended. In a medium bowl, beat egg whites until stiff but not dry. Fold into egg yolk mixture. Generously butter each Aebleskiver cup. Heat according to manufacturer's instructions. Fill each cup 3/4 full with batter. Cook until bubbly and set around edge, about 1-1/2 minutes. Turn 1/4 turn with a fork or wooden pick to brown other side. Continue 1/4 turns each 15 to 30 seconds until lightly browned on all sides and a wooden pick inserted in center comes out clean. Dust with powdered sugar for garnish, if desired. Serve warm. Makes about 20 Aebleskivers.

Variation
After making two 1/4 turns, insert 3 or 4 fresh blueberries into unbaked portion. Continue turning and baking, enclosing berries in center.

1. Generously butter each aebleskiver cup; heat until butter bubbles.

2. With wooden pick or fork, turn muffins 1/4 turn until browned on all sides.

Buttermilk Waffles

All waffles should be like these—light, crisp and golden outside, tender and moist inside.

2-1/2 cups BUTTERMILK
   PANCAKE AND WAFFLE
   MIX, page 13
2 cups water
3 eggs, separated
4 tablespoons vegetable oil

Preheat waffle baker. In a large bowl, combine BUTTER-MILK PANCAKE AND WAFFLE MIX, water, egg yolks and oil. Beat with a wire whisk until just blended. In a medium bowl, beat egg whites until stiff. Fold into egg yolk mixture. Bake according to waffle baker instructions. Makes 3 or 4 large waffles.

Puff Oven Pancakes

Makes a spectacular entrance whenever served.

4 tablespoons butter or
   margarine
4 eggs
2/3 cup milk
2/3 cup BUTTERMILK
   PANCAKE AND WAFFLE
   MIX, page 13
Fiesta Fruit Topping, see below

Fiesta Fruit Topping:
1 (10-oz.) pkg. frozen
   raspberries or strawberries,
   thawed
1 cup pineapple chunks, drained
1 banana, sliced
1/4 cup brown sugar, firmly
   packed
1/4 cup dairy sour cream

Preheat oven to 450F (230C). Put 2 tablespoons butter or margarine each in two 9-inch pie plates. Put in preheating oven to melt butter or margarine. In a blender, combine eggs, milk and BUTTERMILK PANCAKE AND WAFFLE MIX. Pour batter into pie plates. Bake about 18 minutes, until pancakes are puffy and browned. Do not open oven while pancakes are cooking. Top with Fiesta Fruit Topping or your choice of topping. Makes 2 large pancakes.

Fiesta Fruit Topping

Spoon raspberries or strawberries on top of each warm Puff Oven Pancake Top with pineapple chunks and banana. Sprinkle brown sugar over top. Top with teaspoonfuls of sour cream. Serve immediately.

Variation
Tart Lemon Topping: Sprinkle 1-1/2 teaspoons lemon juice over top of each warm Puff Oven Pancake. Sprinkle powdered sugar over top. Serve immediately.

Quick Wheat Breakfast Cake

Serve this cinnamon-nut tidbit on a cold winter morning!

1 egg, slightly beaten
3/4 cup water
2-1/4 cups WHEAT MIX,
  page 14
1 cup chopped raisins
1/2 cup brown sugar, firmly
  packed
2 teaspoons ground cinnamon
1/2 cup chopped nuts

Preheat oven to 375F (190C). Butter an 8-inch square pan. Combine egg and water in a medium bowl. Stir in WHEAT MIX and raisins until moistened. Spread into prepared pan. Combine brown sugar, cinnamon and nuts in a small bowl. Sprinkle on top of cake. Bake 25 to 30 minutes until a toothpick inserted in center comes out clean. Cut into 2-inch squares and serve warm. Makes 16 squares.

Variation
Substitute orange peel and orange juice for part of the water in the recipe.

Favorite Wheat Pancakes

Extra easy and especially nourishing.

1 egg, slightly beaten
1-1/2 cups water
2-1/4 cups WHEAT MIX,
  page 14

Combine egg and water in a medium bowl. Stir in WHEAT MIX until just moistened. Cook on a hot oiled griddle about 3 to 4 minutes, until browned on both sides. Makes about fifteen 4-inch pancakes.

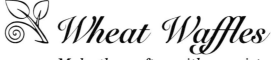

Wheat Waffles

Make these often with a variety of toppings.

2-1/4 cups WHEAT MIX,
  page 14
1-1/3 cups water
3 tablespoons vegetable oil
3 eggs, separated

Preheat waffle baker. In a large bowl, combine WHEAT MIX, water, oil and egg yolks. Beat until just blended. In a medium glass or metal bowl, beat egg whites until stiff. Fold into wheat mixture. Bake according to waffle baker instructions. Makes 3 or 4 large waffles.

# Coffeetime Quick Bread

Delicious toasted and served for breakfast.

1 egg, slightly beaten
1-1/4 cups water
4 cups WHEAT MIX, page 14

Preheat oven to 350F (175C). Grease a 9" x 5" loaf pan. Combine egg and water in a large bowl. Stir in WHEAT MIX until moistened. Turn into prepared pan and bake about 50 minutes, until a toothpick inserted in center comes out clean. Top of loaf should crack. Cool pan on a wire rack about 5 minutes. Loosen sides of bread with a knife and turn right-side up on wire rack. Cool completely before slicing. Makes 1 loaf.

# Sausage Cheese Breakfast Strata

This dish is prepared the night before, then baked in the morning for a wonderful weekend breakfast or brunch.

5 cups HERBED STUFFING
MIX, page 17
1 lb. ground sausage, cooked
and drained
2 cups shredded Cheddar cheese
(8 oz.)
5 eggs, slightly beaten
1 teaspoon dry mustard
2-1/4 cups milk or half-and-half
1 teaspoon salt
Dash of pepper

Lightly grease a 13" x 9" baking pan. Cover bottom of pan with HERBED STUFFING MIX. Add layer of cooked sausage, then layer of cheese. In a medium mixing bowl, combine eggs, mustard, milk or half-and-half, salt and pepper. Pour over cheese. Cover pan and refrigerate overnight. When ready to serve, bake at 325F (165C) for 1 hour. Makes 6 to 8 servings.

English Poached Eggs and Ham

Poach eggs in simmering water or in lightly buttered egg poacher cups.

3 English muffins
1-1/2 cups FREEZER CHEESE
    SAUCE MIX, page 23,
    thawed
6 eggs
6 slices ham
6 cherry tomatoes, for garnish
6 parsley sprigs, for garnish

Cut muffins in half. In broiler or toaster, lightly toast muffin halves. Place each half on a separate plate. In a small saucepan, warm FREEZER CHEESE SAUCE MIX over low heat. Pour water 1-1/2 inches deep in a medium skillet. Bring to a simmer over medium-high heat; do not boil. Break 1 egg into a small bowl or custard cup. Carefully pour egg into simmering water. Cook until egg white is set but tender and egg yolk is slightly set, 3 to 5 minutes. If desired, poach several eggs at once, not letting eggs touch one another. Lift poached eggs from water with a slotted spoon or spatula. Drain on paper towels. Spoon 2 tablespoons of the warmed FREEZER CHEESE SAUCE MIX over each muffin half. Top each with 1 slice ham and 1 poached egg. Spoon remaining sauce evenly over eggs. Garnish each serving with 1 cherry tomato and 1 parsley sprig. Makes 6 servings.

Nevada's Pancakes

Light, crisp and brown outside, moist and tender inside.

2-1/4 cups QUICK MIX, page 11
1 tablespoon sugar
1 egg, beaten
1-1/2 cups milk or water

Combine QUICK MIX and sugar in a medium bowl. Mix well. Combine egg and milk or water in a small bowl. Add all at once to dry ingredients. Blend well. Let stand 5 to 10 minutes. Cook on a hot oiled griddle about 3 to 4 minutes, until browned on both sides. Makes ten to twelve 4-inch pancakes.

Variation
Nevada's Waffles: Bake batter in oiled preheated waffle baker until golden brown. Makes 3 large waffles.

Puffy Omelet

The perfect brunch idea when everyone gets a late start.

1 tablespoon butter or
  margarine
1 cup thinly sliced fresh
  mushrooms
1/2 cup chopped green pepper
6 eggs, separated, room
  temperature
1/8 teaspoon cream of tartar
1/2 teaspoon salt
Pinch pepper
1/3 cup milk
1 tablespoon butter or
  margarine
1 tablespoon vegetable oil
1-1/2 cups FREEZER CHEESE
  SAUCE MIX, page 23,
  thawed
1/2 cup chopped tomatoes

Preheat oven to 350F (175C). In a small skillet, melt 1 tablespoon butter or margarine. Add mushrooms and green pepper. Sauté until crisp-tender. Drain; set aside. In a large bowl, beat egg whites with cream of tartar until stiff peaks form. In a small bowl, beat egg yolks until thick and pale. Gradually beat in salt, pepper and milk until blended. Using a wire whisk, gently fold egg yolk mixture into beaten egg whites. In a large skillet or omelet pan with an oven-proof handle, heat 1 tablespoon butter or margarine and oil until hot, but not browned. Tilt pan to coat sides. Spread egg mixture evenly in pan. Without stirring, cook over low heat until lightly browned on bottom, about 8 minutes. Place skillet or omelet pan in preheated oven. Bake 8 to 10 minutes until top feels somewhat firm when pressed with your fingers. In a small saucepan, heat FREEZER CHEESE SAUCE MIX over low heat, stirring occasionally. Invert omelet onto a large platter. Spoon sauce over omelet. Sprinkle top evenly with tomatoes and sautéed mushrooms and green peppers. Cut in wedges to serve. Makes 4 to 6 servings.

Buttermilk Pancakes

Serve these at a pancake supper with a variety of syrups.

1 egg, beaten
2 tablespoons vegetable oil
About 1 cup water, more if
  desired
1-1/2 cups BUTTERMILK
  PANCAKE AND WAFFLE
  MIX, page 13

In a medium bowl, combine egg, oil and 1 cup water. With a wire whisk, stir in BUTTERMILK PANCAKE AND WAFFLE MIX until blended. Let stand 5 minutes. Stir in additional water for a thinner batter. Preheat griddle according to manufacturer's instructions. Lightly oil griddle. Pour about 1/3 cup batter onto hot griddle to make 1 pancake. Cook until edge is dry and bubbles form. Turn with a wide spatula. Cook 35 to 45 seconds longer until browned on both sides. Repeat with remaining batter. Makes about ten 4-inch pancakes.

Simplified Quiche

Oo-la-la! A French delicacy made easy!

Single Freezer Pie Crust, baked,
    page 33
1 egg, separated
4 strips bacon, partially cooked,
    chopped
1-3/4 cups milk or cream
1 cup shredded Swiss cheese (4
    oz.)
1/2 teaspoon salt
1/4 teaspoon paprika
1 teaspoon minced onion
Dash of cayenne pepper
3 eggs
Chicken gravy, if desired
Pimiento, for garnish

Prepare pie crust in a 9-inch pie plate; set aside to cool. Beat egg white and brush on bottom of pie crust. Reserve egg yolk. Sprinkle bacon evenly over bottom of crust. Scald milk or cream in a medium saucepan. Reduce heat and add shredded cheese. Stir until cheese is melted. Add salt, paprika, onion and cayenne pepper. Remove from heat and cool slightly. Add 3 eggs plus reserved yolk 1 at a time, beating well after each. Pour into pie crust. Bake about 45 minutes, until a toothpick inserted in center comes out clean. Serve with chicken gravy, if desired. Garnish with pimiento. Makes 1 quiche.

Almond Kringle

The filling puffs up and makes a soft, flaky layer.

1 pkg. CREAM CHEESE
    PASTRY MIX, page 34,
    thawed
1/2 cup water
1/4 cup butter or margarine
1/2 cup all-purpose flour
2 eggs
1/4 teaspoon almond extract
Kringle Icing, see below
1/4 cup sliced almonds

Kringle Icing:
1/2 cup powdered sugar
1-1/2 teaspoons cream or milk
2 teaspoons butter or margarine
1/2 teaspoon almond extract

Roll out CREAM CHEESE PASTRY MIX into a 14" x 4" rectangle. Place rolled-out dough on a large baking sheet. Crimp and shape sides of dough to make a raised edge. Preheat oven to 350F (175C). In a small saucepan, combine water and butter or margarine. Bring to a boil over medium-high heat. Add flour all at once, stirring vigorously until mixture forms a ball and leaves side of pan. Remove from heat. Add eggs 1 at a time, beating well after each addition. Beat in almond extract. Spread mixture over pastry. Bake 40 to 45 minutes in preheated oven until golden brown. Cool on a rack 5 minutes. Prepare Kringle Icing. Spread over baked filling. Sprinkle with sliced almonds. To serve, cut in 1-1/2-inch diagonal slices. Makes about 6 servings.

Kringle Icing

In a small bowl, combine all ingredients, beating until smooth.

Breads and Rolls

People often think breads are difficult to make; quick breads aren't quick enough and yeast breads are a scary process! But they're all so easy and delicious when you make them with your own mixes.

Let QUICK MIX and SWEET QUICK BREAD MIX work wonders on those quick breads you don't have time to make the old way. Check the Breakfast and Brunch chapter for additional bread ideas.

Since quick breads are similar to muffins in the proportion of liquid to dry ingredients, be careful not to overbeat them. Stir the batter briskly about 30 seconds and let your oven complete the preparation process.

Did you know biscuits are lighter if the gluten in them is developed a little? You do this by kneading the dough 10 to 15 times. Your biscuits will rise higher and you'll wish you had always made them this way.

HOT ROLL MIX makes it easier for both the beginner and the expert cook to create a wonderful variety of home baked yeast breads and rolls. You will enjoy working with this dough. It is soft, elastic and easy to handle. The aroma and fine texture of your baked products will delight everyone—especially you. Begin with Homemade White Bread and promise yourself you'll try every recipe. The hot rolls come in several shapes you can make all at once. Spread your fresh hot breads and rolls with Honey Butter, page 131.

Now do you feel like the master of your kitchen? Good—treat yourself to some Orange Butterflake Rolls.

Clockwise from top: Crispy Breadsticks, page 131, Homemade White Bread, page 140, Coffeetime Quick Bread, page 120, Indian Fry Bread, page 129, Orange Butterflake Rolls, page 137.

Streusel Topping for Muffins

Sprinkle topping onto muffins of your choice before baking.

1/4 cup chopped pecans or
   walnuts
1/4 cup all-purpose flour
3 tablespoons sugar
2 tablespoons butter or
   margarine, softened
1/4 teaspoon ground cinnamon

Combine all ingredients in a small bowl. Sprinkle 1 to 2 teaspoons onto muffins before baking.

Pan Rolls

Quick, easy and old-fashioned.

1 tablespoon active dry yeast
   (1 (1/4-oz.) package)
1-1/2 cups lukewarm water
   (110F, 45C)
2 eggs, beaten
1/2 cup vegetable oil or melted
   margarine
5 to 6 cups HOT ROLL MIX,
   page 12

In a large bowl, dissolve yeast in lukewarm water. Blend in eggs and oil or margarine. Add 5 cups HOT ROLL MIX. Blend well. Add additional HOT ROLL MIX to make a soft, but not too sticky dough. Knead about 5 minutes, until dough is smooth. Lightly butter bowl. Put dough in bowl and turn to butter top. Cover dough with a damp towel and let rise in a warm place until doubled in bulk, about 1 hour. Grease a 13" x 9" baking pan or two 9-inch round pans. Punch down dough. Divide dough into 24 to 30 balls of equal size. Place balls in prepared pans. Cover and let rise again until doubled in bulk, about 20 to 25 minutes, until golden brown. Makes about 24 rolls.

French Bread

Use one of these loaves to make Savory French Onion Loaves, see below.

1 tablespoon active dry yeast
    (1 (1/4-oz.) package)
1-1/2 cups lukewarm water
    (110F, 45C)
2 eggs, beaten
5 to 6 cups HOT ROLL MIX,
    page 12
1 tablespoon cornmeal
Sesame seeds, if desired
1 to 2 tablespoons butter or
    margarine, melted

In a large bowl, stir yeast into lukewarm water until softened. Stir in eggs. Beat in 5 cups HOT ROLL MIX until blended. Let rest 2 minutes. Stir in enough of the remaining mix to make a soft dough. Knead until smooth, 7 to 10 minutes. Grease bowl. Place dough in bowl, turning to grease all sides. Cover with a damp towel. Let rise in a warm place, free from drafts, until doubled in bulk, about 1 hour. Generously grease 2 baking sheets. Sprinkle with cornmeal; set aside. Punch down dough. On a lightly oiled surface, divide dough into 2 balls. Roll out each ball to one 10" x 3" rectangle. Roll up firmly, jellyroll fashion, starting with one long side. Pinch to seal edges. Place rolled loaves on prepared baking sheet, seam-side down. Make 5 diagonal slashes across top of each loaf. Brush with water. Let rise until almost doubled in bulk. Preheat oven to 375F (190C). Brush loaves again with water. Sprinkle with sesame seeds, if desired. Place a baking pan on lower shelf of oven. Pour 1 inch warm water in pan. Place loaves on a rack in center of oven. Bake 30 to 35 minutes in preheated oven until golden brown. Brush with melted butter. Cool on a rack. Makes 2 loaves.

Savory French Onion Loaves

Grated onion is finer than minced onion and results in a smoother spread.

1 loaf French Bread, see above
French Onion Spread, see below
2 teaspoons dried parsley leaves,
    crushed
2 tablespoons grated Parmesan
    cheese

French Onion Spread:
1/2 cup butter or margarine
2 tablespoons Worcestershire
    sauce
1 cup mayonnaise
1 medium onion, grated

Prepare French Bread; cool completely. Prepare French Onion Spread; set aside. Preheat broiler, if necessary. Cut bread in half lengthwise. Cover cut surfaces with French Onion Spread. Combine parsley and cheese. Sprinkle evenly over spread. Broil 4 to 5 inches from heat source until cheese melts, 30 to 60 seconds. Cut in 2-inch slices. Serve hot. Makes 6 to 8 servings.

French Onion Spread

In a small bowl, cream butter or margarine with Worcestershire sauce and mayonnaise. Stir in grated onion.

Tatonuts

This old-fashioned favorite is easy!

1 tablespoon active dry yeast
 (1 (1/4-oz.) package)
1/2 cup lukewarm water (110F,
 45C)
2 eggs, beaten
1/2 cup melted butter or
 margarine
3 tablespoons sugar
1/2 cup instant potato flakes
1 cup milk, scalded
4-1/2 to 5 cups HOT ROLL
 MIX, page 12
Vegetable oil for frying
Vanilla Glaze, see below

Lightly grease 2 baking sheets. In a large bowl, dissolve yeast in lukewarm water. Stir in eggs and butter or margarine. Add sugar, potato flakes and milk. Blend well. Add 4-1/2 cups HOT ROLL MlX and stir thoroughly. Add additional HOT ROLL MIX to make a soft, but not too sticky dough. Turn out on a lightly floured surface. Knead about 5 minutes, until dough is smooth and satiny. Lightly butter bowl. Put dough in bowl and turn to butter top. Cover dough with a damp towel and let rise in a warm place until doubled in bulk, about 1 hour. Punch down. On a lightly floured surface, roll out dough about 1/4 inch thick. Cut with a floured doughnut cutter. Place on prepared baking sheets. Cover and let rise until doubled in bulk, about 30 to 40 minutes. In a deep-fryer or electric skillet, heat 1/2 inch of oil to 375F (190C). Fry doughnuts about 1 minute on each side until golden brown. Drain on paper towels. While still warm, brush doughnuts with Vanilla Glaze. Makes about 30 doughnuts.

Super-Duper Doughnuts

The spice is nice!

Cooking oil for frying
2 cups QUICK MIX, page 11
1/4 cup sugar
1/4 teaspoon ground cinnamon
1/4 teaspoon ground nutmeg
1 teaspoon vanilla extract
1 egg, well beaten
1/3 cup milk or water
Vanilla Glaze, see below

Vanilla Glaze:
1-1/4 cups powdered sugar
2 teaspoons milk
1/2 teaspoon vanilla extract

In a deep-fryer, heat oil to 375F (190C). In a medium bowl, combine QUICK MIX, sugar, cinnamon and nutmeg. Blend well. In a small bowl, mix together vanilla, egg and milk or water. Add all at once to dry ingredients. Stir until well blended. On a lightly floured surface, knead dough about 10 minutes. Roll out to 1/2-inch thickness and cut with a floured doughnut cutter. Fry in hot oil about l minute on each side, until golden brown. Drain on paper towels. While doughnuts cool slightly, prepare Vanilla Glaze. Dip warm doughnuts in glaze. Makes about 12 doughnuts.

Vanilla Glaze
Combine all ingredients and stir until smooth.

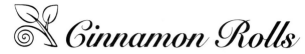

Cinnamon Rolls

The family's favorite. Watch them disappear!

*1 tablespoon active dry yeast
   (1 (1/4-oz.) package)*
*1-1/2 cup lukewarm water
   (110F, 45C)*
2 eggs, beaten
*1/2 cup vegetable oil or melted
   margarine*
*5 to 6 cups HOT ROLL MIX,
   page 12*
Cinnamon Sprinkle, see below
Sweet Glaze, see below

Cinnamon Sprinkle:
*2 tablespoons butter or
   margarine*
*1/2 cup brown sugar, firmly
   packed*
*1-1/2 teaspoons ground
   cinnamon*
1/2 cup raisins
1/4 cup chopped nuts

Sweet Glaze:
1 cup sifted powdered sugar
1/4 teaspoon vanilla extract
About 2 tablespoons milk

In a large bowl, dissolve yeast in lukewarm water. Blend in eggs and oil or margarine. Add 5 cups HOT ROLL MIX. Stir well. Add additional HOT ROLL MIX to make a soft, but not too sticky dough. Knead about 5 minutes, until dough is smooth. Lightly butter bowl. Put dough in bowl and turn to butter top. Cover dough with a damp towel and let rise in a warm place until doubled in bulk, about 1 hour. Generously grease 2 baking sheets. Prepare Cinnamon Sprinkle. Punch down dough. Let stand 10 minutes. On a lightly floured surface, roll out dough to a 12" x 24" rectangle about 1/4 inch thick. Spread generously with Cinnamon Sprinkle. Roll dough like a jellyroll and cut with a sharp knife into twenty-four 1-inch slices. Place on prepared baking sheets. Cover with a damp towel and let rise in a warm place until doubled in bulk, about 30 to 60 minutes. Preheat oven to 375F (190C). Bake 20 to 25 minutes, until golden brown. Prepare Sweet Glaze, and brush on while rolls are still warm. Makes about 24 rolls.

Cinnamon Sprinkle

Melt butter or margarine in a small saucepan. Stir in brown sugar, cinnamon, raisins and nuts.

Sweet Glaze

In a small bowl combine powdered sugar, vanilla and enough milk to make a thin mixture.

Indian Fry Bread

Serve it hot with Honey Butter, page 131, or refried beans.

Vegetable oil for frying
1 cup QUICK MIX, page 11
1/2 cup all-purpose flour
1/4 teaspon salt
About 1/3 cup milk or water

In a deep skillet, heat oil to 375F (190C). In a medium bowl, combine QUICK MIX, flour and salt. Mix well. Add enough milk or water to make a soft dough. On a lightly floured surface, knead about 12 times. Divide into two balls. Pat or roll each ball out to 1/4-inch thickness. Cut into 6 wedges. Fry in hot oil about 2 to 3 minutes until brown on both sides. Drain on paper towels. Makes 12 wedges.

Madeline's Muffins

Sweet and moist with a golden-brown pebbly top.

2-1/2 cups QUICK MIX, page 11
4 tablespoons sugar
1 egg, beaten
1 cup milk or water
Butter and honey, if desired

Preheat oven to 425F (220C). Generously butter muffin pans. Place QUICK MIX in a medium bowl. Add sugar and mix well. In a small bowl, combine egg and milk or water. Add all at once to dry ingredients. Stir until just blended. Fill prepared muffin pans 2/3 full. Bake 15 to 20 minutes, until golden brown. Serve hot with butter and honey, if desired. Makes 12 large muffins.

Variations
Raisin, Date or Nut Muffins: Add 1/2 cup finely chopped raisins, dates or nuts to dry ingredients before adding liquid ingredients. Before baking, sprinkle generously with mixture of cinnamon and sugar.

Blueberry Muffins: Add 1 cup well-drained blueberries to dry ingredients before adding liquid ingredients.

Oatmeal or Bran Muffins: Reduce QUICK MIX to 1-3/4 cups. Add 3/4 cup quick rolled oats or all-bran cereal to dry ingredients before adding liquid ingredients.

Apple Muffins: Add 1 cup grated raw apple to dry ingredients before adding liquid ingredients and increase baking time to 20 to 25 minutes.

Orange Muffins: Add 1 tablespoon fresh orange peel or 1-1/2 teaspoons dehydrated orange peel to dry ingredients before adding liquid ingredients.

Cranberry Muffins: Add 2/3 cup chopped cranberries to dry ingredients before adding liquid ingredients.

Golden Cornbread

Wonderful with chili!

Honey Butter, see below
2 cups QUICK MIX, page 11
6 tablespoons cornmeal
2/3 cup sugar
2 eggs
1 cup milk or water
1/4 cup melted butter or
    margarine

Honey Butter:
1 cup butter, softened
1-1/4 cups honey
1 egg yolk

Prepare Honey Butter. Preheat oven to 350F (175C). Butter a 9-inch square baking pan. Put QUICK MIX, cornmeal and sugar in a medium bowl and stir to blend. Combine eggs with milk or water in a small bowl. Add all at once to dry ingredients. Blend. Add melted butter or margarine and stir to blend. Fill prepared pan. Bake 35 to 40 minutes until golden brown. Cut into 2-1/2 inch squares. Serve hot with Honey Butter. Makes 8 to 10 servings.

Honey Butter

Combine butter, honey and egg yolk in a deep bowl. Beat with electric mixer 10 minutes. Store in refrigerator. Makes about 1-1/2 cups.

Variation
Cornbread Muffins: Butter muffin pans. Fill 3/4 full with cornbread batter. Bake 15 to 20 minutes, until golden brown. Makes 8 to 10 muffins.

Crispy Breadsticks

Add crispy crunch to your Italian dishes.

1 cup QUICK MIX, page 11
1/4 cup cornmeal or all-purpose
    flour
1/4 teaspoon salt
About 1/4 cup milk or water
Sesame or poppy seeds, if
    desired

Preheat oven to 400F (205C). Lightly grease baking sheet. In a medium bowl, combine QUICK MIX, cornmeal or flour, and salt. Add milk or water to form dough. Knead about 12 times, until dough is smooth. Shape into pencil-like strands 1/2 inch thick. Cut into 8- to 10-inch lengths. Roll in sesame or poppy seeds, if desired. Bake about 20 minutes, until brown and crisp. For extra crispness, turn off oven and leave breadsticks in oven 5 to 10 more minutes. Makes 6 breadsticks.

Karine's Drop Biscuits

When time is short, try this simplified biscuit recipe.

3 cups QUICK MIX, page 11
3/4 cup milk or water

Preheat oven to 450F (230C). Grease a baking sheet. Combine QUICK MIX and milk or water in a medium bowl. Stir until just blended. Drop dough by tablespoonfuls onto prepared baking sheet. Bake 10 to 12 minutes, until golden brown. Makes 12 large drop biscuits.

Variations
Cheese and Herb Biscuits: Add 1/3 cup grated Cheddar cheese and chopped parsley, chives or herbs to taste while stirring dough.

Buttermilk Biscuits: Substitute 3/4 cup buttermilk for milk or water.

Country Dumplings: Drop dough by tablespoonfuls over top of boiling beef or chicken stew. Boil gently 10 minutes, uncovered. Cover and cook over medium-high heat 10 more minutes, until cooked through. Makes 12 dumplings.

Orange Biscuits: Add 1 tablespoon grated orange peel. If desired, substitute 2 tablespoons orange juice for part of milk or water.

Fruit Cobbler: Spoon dough over top of hot, sweetened fruit or berries and bake in an 8-inch square pan about 20 to 25 minutes until golden brown.

Never-Fail Rolled Biscuits

These light biscuits separate into layers.

3 cups QUICK MIX, page 11
2/3 cup milk or water

Preheat oven to 450F (230C). Combine QUICK MIX and milk or water in a medium bowl. Blend. Let dough stand 5 minutes. On a lightly floured board, knead dough about 15 times. Roll out to 1/2 inch thickness. Cut with a floured biscuit cutter. Place about 2 inches apart on unbuttered baking sheet. Bake 10 to 12 minutes, until golden brown. Makes 12 large biscuits.

Variations

Cinnamon Rolls: Preheat oven to 400F (205C). Roll out dough to a rectangle. Brush with melted butter. Sprinkle with brown sugar and cinnamon. Roll dough like a jelly-roll and cut into 1/2-inch slices. Bake 10 to 15 minutes. Glaze with mixture of powdered sugar and a few drops of water.

Pizza: Use dough as crust for 12 individual pizzas or two 12-inch pizzas. Pat dough to 1/8-inch thickness. Top with tomato sauce, spices, cheese, meat and choice of toppings.

Meat Pinwheels: Preheat oven to 450F (230C). Roll out dough to a rectangle. Chop cooked meat and combine with gravy. Spread over dough. Roll dough like a jellyroll and cut into 1/2-inch slices. Bake 10 to 12 minutes. Serve with gravy, soup or cheese sauce.

Pot Pie: Use as the top crust of a chicken or meat pot pie.

Cream Cheese Swirls

A real bake shop treat.

1 tablespoon active dry yeast
  (1 (1/4-oz.) package)
1-1/2 cups lukewarm water
  (110F, 45C)
2 eggs, beaten
1/2 cup vegetable oil or melted
  margarine
5 to 6 cups HOT ROLL MIX,
  page 12
Sugar-Cinnamon Sprinkle, see
  below
Cream Cheese Filling, see below
Sweet Glaze, see below

Sugar-Cinnamon Sprinkle:
2 tablespoons butter or
  margarine, melted
1/2 cup brown sugar, firmly
  packed
1-1/2 teaspoons ground
  cinnamon

Cream Cheese Filling:
1 (8-oz.) pkg. cream cheese,
  softened
6 tablespoons sugar
1 egg, slightly beaten
1/2 teaspoon vanilla extract

Sweet Glaze:
1 cup sifted powdered sugar
1/4 teaspoon vanilla extract
About 2 tablespoons milk

In a large bowl, dissolve yeast in lukewarm water. Blend in eggs and oil or margarine. Add 5 cups HOT ROLL MIX. Stir well. Add additional HOT ROLL MIX to make a soft, but not too sticky dough. Knead about 5 minutes, until dough is smooth. Lightly butter bowl. Put dough in bowl and turn to butter top. Cover dough with a damp towel and let rise in a warm place until doubled in bulk, about 1 hour. Generously grease 2 baking sheets. Prepare Sugar-Cinnamon Sprinkle and Cream Cheese Filling. Punch down dough. Let stand 10 minutes. On a lightly floured surface, roll out dough to a 12" x 24" rectangle, about 1/4 inch thick. Spread generously with Sugar-Cinnamon Sprinkle. Roll dough like a jellyroll. Cut into 1-inch slices. Place on prepared baking sheets. Cover with a damp towel and let rise in a warm place until doubled in bulk, about 30 to 60 minutes. Preheat oven to 375F (190C). With a tablespoon, press a deep indentation in the center of each bun. Fill the indentation with 3 tablespoons Cream Cheese Filling. Bake 20 to 25 minutes, until golden brown. Prepare Sweet Glaze. Drizzle glaze on warm buns. Makes about 24 rolls.

Sugar-Cinnamon Sprinkle
Combine all ingredients in a small bowl.

Cream Cheese Filling
In a small bowl cream together cream cheese and sugar until smooth. Add egg and vanilla. Mix well.

Sweet Glaze
In a small bowl combine powdered sugar, vanilla and enough milk to make a thin mixture.

Butterscotch Butter Balls

A melt-in-your-mouth specialty.

1 tablespoon active dry yeast
    (1 (1/4-oz.) package)
1-1/2 cups lukewarm water
    (110F, 45C)
2 eggs, beaten
1/2 cup vegetable oil or melted
    margarine
5 to 6 cups HOT ROLL MIX,
    page 12
1 (3-oz.) pkg. regular
    butterscotch pudding
1 cup butter or margarine,
    melted
1 cup brown sugar, firmly
    packed
1 (1-1/2-oz.) pkg. pecans,
    chopped
2 teaspoons ground cinnamon

In a large bowl, dissolve yeast in lukewarm water. Blend in eggs and oil or margarine. Add 5 cups of HOT ROLL MIX. Stir well. Add additional HOT ROLL MIX to make a soft, but not too sticky dough. Knead about 5 minutes, until dough is smooth. Lightly butter bowl. Put dough in bowl and turn to butter top. Cover dough with a damp towel and let rise in a warm place until doubled in bulk, about 1 hour. Punch down dough. Divide dough into 48 balls of equal size. Place balls on a baking sheet. Cover with plastic wrap and freeze. When frozen, transfer to plastic bags for storage in freezer. Use within 1 to 2 months. About 8 hours before serving, or the night before, place 24 frozen balls in each of 2 unbuttered bundt pans. Sprinkle half of butterscotch pudding on each pan of frozen rolls. Combine melted butter or margarine and brown sugar in a small bowl. Pour half of mixture over each pan of rolls. Sprinkle half of pecans and half of cinnamon over each pan. Cover both pans with towels and let rise about 8 hours or overnight. Preheat oven to 350F (175C). Bake about 30 minutes, until golden brown. Makes 2 butterscotch rings.

1. Divide the dough into 48 balls and place the balls on cookie sheets. Cover with plastic wrap and freeze.

2. Place 24 frozen balls in each bundt pan. Sprinkle butterscotch pudding over the balls, then pour the mixture of butter or margarine and brown sugar over each pan of rolls.

 *Pluckit*

A fun pull-apart bread for snack or mealtime.

1 tablespoon active dry yeast (1
    (1/4-oz.) package)
1-1/2 cups lukewarm water
    (110F, 45C)
2 eggs, beaten
1/2 cup vegetable oil or melted
    margarine
5 to 6 cups HOT ROLL MIX,
    page 12
3 teaspoons ground cinnamon
3/4 cup sugar
1/2 cup butter or margarine,
    melted

In a large bowl, dissolve yeast in lukewarm water. Blend in eggs and oil or margarine. Add 5 cups of HOT ROLL MIX. Stir well. Add additional HOT ROLL MIX to make a soft, but not too sticky dough. Knead about 5 minutes, until dough is smooth. Lightly butter bowl. Put dough in bowl and turn to butter top. Cover dough with a damp towel and let rise in a warm place until doubled in bulk, about 1 hour. Punch down dough. Roll dough into balls about the size of a walnut. Combine cinnamon and sugar in a small bowl. Dip balls in melted butter or margarine and roll in cinnamon-sugar mixture. Pile loosely into an unbuttered tube pan. Let rise until doubled in bulk, about 30 minutes. Preheat oven to 400F (205C). Bake about 10 minutes. Lower temperature to 350F (175C) and continue baking 30 minutes until golden. Loosen edges with a knife and turn out onto a plate. Rolls can be plucked off one at a time. Makes 1 large pan of rolls.

Variation
To make a coffee cake, roll the balls of dough in cinnamon-sugar mixture, then in 1/2 cup chopped nuts.

Orange Butterflake Rolls

A touch of citrus adds a delightful taste!

1 tablespoon active dry yeast
  (1 (1/4-oz.) package)
1-1/2 cups lukewarm water
  (110F, 45C)
2 eggs, beaten
1/2 cup vegetable oil or melted
  margarine
5 to 6 cups HOT ROLL MIX,
  page 12
Orange Butter, see below
Orange Glaze, see below

Orange Butter:
2 tablespoons butter or
  margarine, melted
1/2 cup sugar
2 tablespoons grated orange peel

Orange Glaze:
1 cup sifted powdered sugar
About 2 tablespoons orange
  juice

In a large bowl, dissolve yeast in lukewarm water. Blend in eggs and oil or margarine. Add 5 cups HOT ROLL MIX. Blend well. Add additional HOT ROLL MIX to make a soft, but not too sticky dough. Knead about 5 minutes, until dough is smooth. Lightly butter bowl. Put dough in bowl and turn to butter top. Cover dough with a damp towel and let rise in a warm place until doubled in bulk, about 1 hour. Generously grease muffin pans. Prepare Orange Butter. Punch down dough. Let stand 10 minutes. On a lightly floured surface, roll out dough to a 10" x 20" rectangle. Brush with Orange Butter. Cut into twenty 1" x 10" strips. Stack 5 strips together. Cut each stack into 6 equal pieces. Place each cut stack upright in prepared muffin pans. Cover and let rise again until doubled in bulk, about 30 minutes. Preheat oven to 400F (205C). Bake 15 to 20 minutes, until golden brown. Prepare Orange Glaze, and brush on while rolls are still warm. Makes about 24 rolls.

Orange Butter
Combine butter, sugar and orange peel.

Orange Glaze
Blend powdered sugar and orange juice until smooth.

Mary's Honey-Walnut Swirl

The compliments will be as sweet as the bread!

2 tablespoons active dry yeast
(2 (1/4-oz.) packages)
1 cup lukewarm water (110F,
45C)
2 eggs, beaten
1 cup water
4 tablespoons vegetable oil
1 teaspoon grated orange peel
1 teaspoon grated lemon peel
6-1/2 to 7 cups HOT ROLL
MIX, page 12
Honey Filling, see below
Powdered Sugar Glaze, page
116

Honey Filling:
3/4 cup sugar
1/4 cup honey
1 egg, beaten
1/2 teaspoon vanilla extract
1 teaspoon ground cinnamon
1/4 teaspoon salt
1/2 cup chopped nuts

In a large bowl, dissolve yeast in 1 cup lukewarm water. When yeast starts to bubble, add eggs, 1 cup water, oil, orange peel and lemon peel. Blend well. Add HOT ROLL MIX 1 cup at a time to make a soft dough. On a lightly floured surface, knead dough 5 to 7 minutes, until smooth and satiny. Lightly butter bowl. Put dough in bowl and turn to butter top. Cover with a damp towel and let rise in a warm place until doubled in bulk, about 1 hour. Punch down dough. Prepare Honey Filling. Preheat oven to 375F (190C). Butter two 9" x 5" loaf pans. Divide dough into 2 balls. Roll out each ball to two 9" x 14" rectangles, about 1/2 inch thick. Spread Honey Filling to within 1 inch of edges. Roll up like a jellyroll from small end, lifting dough slightly and sealing edges as you roll. Seal ends and put into prepared pans, seam-side down. Cover and let rise in a warm place until dough is slightly rounded above top of pan. Bake 45 to 50 minutes, until deep golden brown. Cool on a wire rack. While still warm, drizzle Powdered Sugar Glaze on top of loaves. Makes 2 loaves.

Honey Filling
Combine all ingredients in a small bowl. Blend well.

1. *On a lightly floured surface, knead the yeast dough 5 to 7 minutes until smooth and satiny.*

2. *Spread the filling to within 1 inch of the edges of the dough rectangles. Then roll the dough like a jellyroll.*

3. *While the baked loaves are still warm, drizzle Powdered Sugar Glaze over the top of each.*

Crescent Rolls

Buttery, rich and golden.

1 tablespoon active dry yeast
  (1 (1/4-oz.) package)
1-1/2 cups lukewarm water
  (110F, 45C)
2 eggs, beaten
1/2 cup vegetable oil or melted
  margarine
5 to 6 cups HOT ROLL MIX,
  page 12
2 tablespoons butter or
  margarine, softened

In a large bowl, dissolve yeast in lukewarm water. Blend in eggs and oil or margarine. Add 5 cups HOT ROLL MIX. Blend well. Add additional HOT ROLL MIX to make a soft, but not too sticky dough. Knead about 5 minutes, until dough is smooth. Lightly butter bowl. Put dough in bowl and turn to butter top. Cover dough with a damp towel and let rise in a warm place until doubled in bulk, about 1 hour. Generously grease baking sheets. Punch down dough. Divide in half. Let stand 10 minutes. On a lightly floured surface, roll out each half to a 12-inch circle. Brush each circle with 1 tablespoon soft butter or margarine. Cut each circle into 16 pie-shaped wedges. Roll up each wedge from the wide end. Place point-side down in a crescent shape on prepared baking sheets. Cover and let rise again until doubled in bulk, about 45 to 60 minutes. Preheat oven to 400F (205C). Bake 15 to 20 minutes, until golden brown. Makes about 32 rolls.

Homemade White Bread

This will remind you of Grandma's homemade bread, but you'll make it faster.

2 tablespoons active dry yeast
  (1 (1/4-oz.) package)
1 cup lukewarm water (110F,
  45C)
2 eggs, beaten
1 cup water
4 tablespoons vegetable oil
6-1/2 to 7 cups HOT ROLL
  MIX, page 12
Butter or margarine

In a large bowl, dissolve yeast in lukewarm water. When yeast starts to bubble, add eggs, water and oil. Blend well. Add HOT ROLL MIX 1 cup at a time, until dough is stiff. On a lightly floured surface, knead dough 5 to 7 minutes, until smooth and satiny. Lightly butter bowl. Put dough in bowl and turn to butter top. Cover with damp towel and let rise in a warm place until doubled in bulk, about 45 to 60 minutes. Punch down dough. Let stand 10 minutes. Shape into 2 loaves. Grease two 9" x 5" loaf pans. Place 1 loaf of dough in each pan, seam-side down. Cover and let rise again until slightly rounded above top of pan, about 30 to 40 minutes. Preheat oven to 375F (190C). Bake 45 to 55 minutes, until deep golden brown. Remove from oven and brush tops with butter or margarine. Remove from pans and cool on a wire rack. Makes 2 loaves.

Variation
Raisin Bread: Add 1 cup raisins with HOT ROLL MIX. Toast bread, if desired.

Giant Braided Loaf

See the variation below for shaping the dough into pan loaves.

1 tablespoon active dry yeast
(1 (1/4-oz.) package)
1-1/2 cups lukewarm water
(110F, 45C)
2 eggs, beaten
1/2 cup butter or margarine,
melted, or 1/2 cup vegetable
oil
5 to 6 cups HOT ROLL MIX,
page 12
1 egg yolk
1 tablespoon water
1 tablespoon caraway, sesame or
poppy seeds
1 tablespoon butter or
margarine, melted

In a large bowl, stir yeast into lukewarm water until softened. Stir in 2 beaten eggs and 1/2 cup melted butter or margarine or oil. Beat in 5 cups HOT ROLL MIX. Let rest 2 minutes. Add enough of the remaining mix to make a soft dough. Turn out on a lightly floured surface. Knead until smooth, 7 to 10 minutes. Grease bowl. Place dough in bowl, turning to grease all sides. Cover with a damp towel. Let rise in a warm place, free from drafts, until doubled in bulk. Grease 1 large baking sheet; set aside. Punch down dough. Let rest 10 minutes. Divide into 4 equal pieces. Shape 3 pieces into 15-inch ropes. Arrange ropes about 1 inch apart on greased baking sheet. Braid loosely from center to either end. Pinch ends together. Divide remaining piece of dough into 3 equal pieces. Shape each into a 12-inch rope. Braid as directed above. Place on top of large braid, pinching ends of small braid into large braid. In a small bowl, combine 1 egg yolk and 1 tablespoon water. Brush over braids. Sprinkle with caraway, sesame or poppy seeds. Cover and let rise until almost doubled in bulk. Preheat oven to 375F (190C). Bake 40 to 50 minutes until deep golden brown. Brush tops with 1 tablespoon melted butter or margarine. Cool on a rack. Makes 1 large loaf.

Variation

Loaves: Divide dough into 2 equal pieces. Roll out each piece into a 12" x 8" rectangle. Roll up each rectangle jellyroll fashion, starting with a short side. Pinch ends together to seal. Place each shaped loaf in a greased 9" x 5" loaf pan, seam-side down. Cover and let rise until slightly rounded above the tops of pans. Bake as directed above.

Hamburger Buns

Make hot dog buns by shaping the dough into logs.

2 tablespoons active dry yeast
  (1 (1/4-oz.) package)
1-1/2 cups lukewarm water
  (110F, 45C)
2 eggs, beaten
1/2 cup vegetable oil
5 to 6 cups HOT ROLL MIX,
  page 12
2 tablespoons butter or
  margarine, melted

In a large bowl, stir yeast into lukewarm water until softened. Stir in eggs and oil. Beat in 5 cups of the HOT ROLL MIX until blended. Let rest 2 minutes. Add enough of the remaining mix to make a soft dough. Knead until smooth, 7 to 10 minutes. Grease bowl. Place dough in bowl, turning to grease all sides. Cover with a damp towel. Let rise in a warm place, free from drafts, until doubled in bulk. Grease 2 baking sheets; set aside. Punch down dough. Let rest 10 minutes. Use a rolling pin to roll out dough 1/2-inch thick. Cut buns with a large can or bun cutter, or divide dough into 12 equal pieces, shaping each into a 4-inch circle, 1/2 inch thick. Let rise 10 to 15 minutes. Preheat oven to 425F (220C). Bake 10 minutes until golden brown. Remove from baking sheets; cool on a rack. To keep the buns soft, brush with butter or margarine then cover with a dry cloth. Makes twelve 5-inch buns.

Melt-in-Your-Mouth Muffins

A delicious addition to bacon and eggs.

2-3/4 cups MUFFIN MIX,
    page 13
1 egg, beaten
1 cup milk
1/2 cup butter or margarine,
    melted, or 1/2 cup vegetable
    oil

Preheat oven to 400F (205C). Butter muffin pans. Put MUF-FIN MIX in a medium bowl. Combine egg, milk and butter, margarine or oil in a small bowl. Add all at once to MUFFIN MIX. Stir until mix is just moistened; batter should be lumpy. Fill prepared muffin pans 3/4 full. Bake 18 to 20 minutes, until golden brown. Makes 10 large muffins.

Variations
Corn Meal Muffins: Decrease MUFFIN MIX to 2-1/4 cups. Add 1/2 cup cornmeal.

Jelly Muffins: Fill each muffin cup 1/3 full with batter. Drop 1 teaspoon jelly on top of batter. Fill cups 3/4 full with batter.

Butterscotch-Pecan Muffins: Melt 6 tablespoons butter or margarine in a small saucepan. Stir in 6 tablespoons brown sugar. Place 1 tablespoon of brown sugar mixture and 2 to 3 pecans in bottom of each muffin cup. Fill cups 3/4 full with batter.

Apricot Muffins: Add 1 cup chopped dried apricots to liquid ingredients before adding liquid to MUFFIN MIX.

Banana Muffins: Mash 1 large banana (1/2 cup) and add to liquid ingredients before adding liquid to MUFFIN MIX.

Blueberry Muffins: Add 1 cup well-drained blueberries to liquid ingredients before adding liquid to MUFFIN MIX.

Molasses Bran Muffins

A rich tea or breakfast muffin—well worth the extra effort.

Pan Coating, see below
1-1/4 cups MUFFIN MIX,
    page 13
2 cups bran cereal
1/2 teaspoon baking soda
1/4 cup molasses
1 egg, beaten
1 cup buttermilk
1 (8-oz.) can crushed pineapple,
    drained
3/4 cup raisins, if desired

Pan Coating:
1/4 cup butter or margarine,
    softened
1/4 cup sugar
1/4 cup brown sugar, firmly
    packed
1 tablespoon honey
1/4 cup chopped pecans

Prepare Pan Coating. Set aside. Preheat oven to 400F (205C). In a medium bowl, combine MUFFIN MIX, cereal, baking soda, molasses, egg, buttermilk, pineapple and raisins, if desired. Stir until just moistened. Fill prepared muffin pan 3/4 full. Bake 15 to 20 minutes until edges are brown. Remove immediately from oven and invert on cooling rack. Spoon any remaining topping back to the bottom of muffin. Makes 12 muffins.

Pan Coating

In a small bowl, cream together butter or margarine and sugars. Stir in honey and pecans. Spoon heaping teaspoon into each muffin cup.

Cornmeal Muffins

Family members won't need coaxing to eat these delights.

2-1/4 cups MUFFIN MIX, page
    13
1/2 cup cornmeal
1/2 cup melted butter or
    margarine or oil
1 egg, beaten
1 cup milk

Preheat oven to 400F (205C). Butter muffin pans. Put MUFFIN MIX and cornmeal in a medium bowl. Blend well. Combine butter or margarine or oil, egg and milk in a small bowl. Add all at once to muffin mixture. Stir until just moistened; batter should be lumpy. Fill prepared muffin pans 3/4 full. Bake 18 to 20 minutes until golden brown. Makes 10 large muffins.

Clockwise from top left: Cornmeal Muffins, page 145, Molasses Bran Muffins with Raisins, page 145, Melt-in-Your-Mouth Muffins with Apricots, page 143.

Apple Muffins

The best way to have an apple a day.

2-3/4 cups MUFFIN MIX,
    page 13
1/2 cup chopped nuts
1/2 teaspoon ground cloves
2 cups grated apples
1 egg, beaten
1/2 cup melted butter or
    margarine or oil
1 cup milk

Preheat oven to 400F (205C). Butter muffin pans. In a medium bowl, combine MUFFIN MIX, nuts and cloves. Combine apples, egg and butter, margarine or oil and milk in a medium bowl. Add all at once to dry ingredients. Stir until just moistened; batter should be lumpy. Fill prepared muffin pans 3/4 full. Bake 18 to 20 minutes until golden brown. Makes 10 large muffins.

Quick Wheat Muffins

Serve hot. How yummy!

3 cups WHEAT MIX, page 14
2 tablespoons sugar
1 egg, slightly beaten
1 cup water

Preheat oven to 400F (205C). Generously butter muffin pans. In a medium bowl, combine WHEAT MIX and sugar. Blend well. Combine egg and water in a small bowl. Add all at once to dry ingredients. Stir until just moistened; batter should be lumpy. Fill prepared muffin pans 2/3 full. Bake 15 to 20 minutes, until golden brown. Makes 12 large muffins.

Banana-Nut Bread

Freeze overripe bananas in peel. Thaw, then mash just before using.

3-3/4 cups SWEET QUICK
    BREAD MIX, page 15
2 eggs, beaten
1 tablespoon lemon juice
2 medium bananas, mashed
    (about 1 cup)
1/2 cup chopped nuts

Preheat oven to 325F (165C). Grease one 9" x 5" loaf pan or two 7" x 3" loaf pans; set aside. In a medium bowl, combine all ingredients, stirring to blend. Turn into prepared pan or pans. Bake 50 to 60 minutes in preheated oven until a wooden pick inserted in center comes out clean. Cool on a rack 5 minutes. Turn out of pan. Cool right-side up on rack. Makes 1 or 2 loaves.

Carrot-Orange Loaf

When cool, serve with Cinnamon Whipped Topping from Pumpkin Bread, page 148.

3-3/4 cups SWEET QUICK
    BREAD MIX, page 15
2 eggs, beaten
1 cup grated carrots
1/2 cup orange juice
1 teaspoon grated orange peel
1 teaspoon ground nutmeg
1 teaspoon ground cinnamon
1/2 cup chopped nuts
1/2 cup raisins

Preheat oven to 325F (165C). Grease one 9" x 5" loaf pan or two 7" x 3" loaf pans; set aside. In a medium bowl, combine all ingredients, stirring to blend. Turn into prepared pan or pans. Bake 60 to 70 minutes in preheated oven until a wooden pick inserted in center comes out clean. Cool on a rack 5 minutes. Turn out of pan. Cool right-side up on rack. Makes 1 or 2 loaves.

Variation
Substitute 1 (7-1/2-ounce) jar junior baby-food carrots for grated carrots and orange juice.

Cranberry Bread

Freeze fresh cranberries when they are in season so you can make this bread all year.

3/4 cup orange juice
1 cup fresh or frozen cranberries
2 eggs, beaten
3-3/4 cups SWEET QUICK
    BREAD MIX, page 15
1 teaspoon grated orange peel

Preheat oven to 325F (165C). Grease one 9" x 5" loaf pan or two 7" x 3" loaf pans; set aside. Combine orange juice and cranberries in blender. Process on chop 4 or 5 seconds. In a medium bowl, combine eggs, SWEET QUICK BREAD MIX, orange peel and orange juice mixture, stirring to blend. Turn into prepared pan or pans. Bake 65 to 75 minutes in preheated oven until a wooden pick inserted in center comes out clean. Cool on a rack 5 minutes. Turn out of pan or pans. Cool right-side up on rack. Makes 1 or 2 loaves.

Date-Nut Bread

For a different shape, bake this bread in a Bundt pan at 325F (165C) for about 1 hour.

1 cup boiling water
1 cup chopped dates
2 eggs, beaten
3-3/4 cups SWEET QUICK
 BREAD MIX, page 15
1 teaspoon vanilla extract
1/2 cup chopped nuts

Preheat oven to 350F (175C). Grease one 9" x 5" loaf pan or two 7" x 3" loaf pans; set aside. In a small bowl, pour boiling water over dates. Let stand 5 minutes. In a medium bowl, combine eggs, SWEET QUICK BREAD MIX, vanilla and nuts, stirring to blend. Stir in date mixture. Turn into prepared pan or pans. Bake 60 to 65 minutes in preheated oven until a wooden pick inserted in center comes out clean. Cool on a rack 5 minutes. Turn out of pan or pans. Cool right-side up on rack. Makes 1 or 2 loaves.

Pumpkin Bread

Serve the Cinnamon Whipped Topping with any sweet quick bread.

3-3/4 cups SWEET QUICK
 BREAD MIX, page 15
1 cup mashed cooked pumpkin
2 eggs, beaten
1/2 cup milk
1/2 teaspoon ground cinnamon
1/2 teaspoon ground nutmeg
1/2 teaspoon ground cloves
1/2 cup chopped nuts
1/2 cup raisins
Cinnamon Whipped Topping,
 see below

Cinnamon Whipped Topping:
1 cup whipping cream
1 teaspoon ground cinnamon
3 tablespoons powdered sugar

Preheat oven to 350F (175C). Grease one 9" x 5" loaf pan or two 7" x 3" loaf pans; set aside. In a medium bowl, combine SWEET QUICK BREAD MIX, pumpkin, eggs, milk, cinnamon, nutmeg and cloves, stirring to blend. Stir in nuts and raisins. Turn into prepared pan or pans. Bake 55 to 60 minutes in preheated oven until a wooden pick inserted in center comes out clean. Cool on a rack 5 minutes. Turn out of pan. Prepare topping. Cool right-side up on rack. To serve, cut into 1/2-inch slices; spread each with Cinnamon Whipped Topping. Makes 1 or 2 loaves.

Cinnamon Whipped Topping

In a medium bowl, whip cream until soft peaks form. Gently stir in cinnamon and powdered sugar. Refrigerate until served. Makes about 2 cups.

Spicy Applesauce Bread

Spread cooled slices with whipped cream cheese.

3-3/4 cups SWEET QUICK
    BREAD MIX, page 15
2 eggs, beaten
1-1/2 teaspoons ground
    cinnamon
1/2 teaspoon ground allspice
1/2 teaspoon ground cloves
1 cup applesauce
1/2 cup chopped nuts
1/2 cup raisins

Preheat oven to 325F (165C). Grease one 9" x 5" loaf pan or two 7" x 3" loaf pans; set aside. In a medium bowl, combine all ingredients, stirring to blend. Turn into prepared pan or pans. Bake 60 to 75 minutes in preheated oven until a wooden pick inserted in center comes out clean. Cool on a rack 5 minutes. Turn out of pan or pans. Cool right-side up on rack. Makes 1 or 2 loaves.

Zucchini Bread

To prevent tunnels in your bread, stir only until all the ingredients are moistened.

3-3/4 cups SWEET QUICK
    BREAD MIX, page 15
2 eggs, beaten
2 cups grated unpeeled zucchini
    squash
3 tablespoons orange juice
1 teaspoon grated orange peel
1/2 cup chopped nuts

Preheat oven to 325F (165C). Grease one 9" x 5" loaf pan or two 7" x 3" loaf pans; set aside. In a medium bowl, combine all ingredients, stirring to blend. Turn into prepared pan or pans. Bake 60 to 75 minutes in preheated oven until a wooden pick inserted in center comes out clean. Cool on a rack 5 minutes. Turn out of pan. Cool right-side up on rack. Makes 1 or 2 loaves.

Cakes and Pies

Don't want the fuss and mess of making a cake from "scratch"? Try the ultimate dessert convenience—SNACK CAKE MIX, page 14. Although the recipes which use this mix describe two steps for the convenience of beginners, you can mix all of the ingredients in the baking pan to save time, effort and dishwashing. Most of the cakes do not need frosting or create their own frosting while baking. The Carrot Snack Cake gives you the option of substituting a jar of junior baby food carrots for the grated carrots in the recipe, making it even easier to prepare.

Keep several packages of FREEZER PIE CRUST MIX, page 32, in your freezer. Directions for preparing dough for single or double-crust pies are with the mix. When fresh fruit is in season and FREEZER PIE CRUST MIX is in the freezer, fresh homemade fruit pies can be minutes away. Try some of our pie recipes such as All-American Apple Pie with Hot Butter Sauce. Try our pie crust with some of your favorite pies as well.

Turnover Fried Pies

Main dish or dessert. You choose by the filling you use.

Vegetable oil for frying
2 cups QUICK MIX, page 11
1/2 cup milk or water
Fruit Fillings, see below
Main Dish Fillings, see below

Preheat 1 inch of oil to 350F (175C) in an electric skillet. Combine QUICK MIX and milk or water in a medium bowl. Stir to blend. On a lightly floured surface, knead about 15 times, until dough is smooth. Roll dough as for pie crust. Cut into 5-inch diameter circles. Place 1 to 2 tablespoons of filling on half of each circle. Fold dough over and press the edges firmly with fork tines dipped in flour. Fry in hot oil about 2 minutes on each side, until golden brown. Makes 8 to 10 turnover pies.

Fruit Fillings

Applesauce: Fill with thick, flavored applesauce.

Fresh Fruit: Fill with fresh, cut-up, sweetened fruit such as strawberries, peaches, apricots or raspberries.

Canned Pie Fillings: Fill with any fruit pie filling such as cherry, blueberry or lemon.

Dried Fruit: Fill with cooked dried apricots, peaches or apples with 3 tablespoons sugar added to fruit mixture.

Pineapple: Fill with mixture of 2/3 cup drained, crushed pineapple, 4 teaspoons sugar and 2 teaspoons cornstarch, cooked together until thickened, then cooled.

Mincemeat: Fill with mixture of equal parts mincemeat and thick applesauce.

Main Dish Fillings

Chili: Fill with thick homemade or canned chili.

Chicken or Tuna: Fill with mixture of 1 cup minced, cooked chicken or tuna, 1 tablespoon chopped pimiento or parsley and 1/4 cup chicken gravy or cream of chicken soup.

Runza: Fill with mixture of 1/4 cup minced onion and 1/4 pound lean ground beef, browned together and combined with 1 cup shredded cabbage, 1/2 teaspoon salt and pepper to taste. Cook together 5 minutes and drain before filling pies.

Pineapple Upside-Down Cake

A light, moist cake with a tangy fruit topping.

Brown Sugar Topping, see below
3 cups QUICK MIX, page 11
1-1/3 cups sugar
1 cup milk
3 eggs, slightly beaten
1-1/2 teaspoons vanilla extract
1 (20-oz.) can crushed pineapple, drained

Brown Sugar Topping:
1 cup brown sugar, firmly packed
1/2 cup butter or margarine

Lightly butter a 13" x 9" baking pan or two 8-inch square pans. Prepare Brown Sugar Topping and set aside. Preheat oven to 350F (175C). Combine QUICK MIX and sugar in a large bowl. Mix well. In a small bowl, combine milk, eggs and vanilla. Add half of milk mixture to dry ingredients. Beat 2 minutes until batter is smooth. Add remaining milk mixture, and beat 2 to 3 more minutes. Distribute Brown Sugar Topping evenly over bottom of pan. Spoon crushed pineapple smoothly over topping. Spread batter over pineapple. Bake 45 to 50 minutes, until center springs back when lightly touched. Cool in pan 10 minutes, then invert onto a serving plate. Serve warm with pineapple side up. Makes one large cake or two 8-inch cakes.

Brown Sugar Topping

In a small bowl, combine brown sugar and butter or margarine until mixture is evenly distributed.

Variation
Substitute frozen or canned fruit, thawed and drained, for pineapple. Try peaches, apples, apricots, strawberries or raspberries. If using strawberries or raspberries, substitute granulated sugar for brown sugar.

1. Pat the mixture of brown sugar and butter or margarine evenly over the bottom of two 8-inch square pans or one 13'' x 9'' pan. Spoon crushed pineapple over mixture.

2. Use a rubber scraper to spread the batter mixture evenly over the Pineapple Topping.

3. Cool the cake 10 minutes in the pan, then invert onto a serving plate. Serve it warm, upside-down.

Cranberry Cakes with Butter Sauce

The hot butter sauce compliments the tart cranberries in this fall dessert.

1 cup raw cranberries, chopped
1/4 cup sugar
2-3/4 cups MUFFIN MIX,
　　page 13
1 cup dairy sour cream
1 egg, beaten
1/4 cup butter or margarine or
　　oil
Hot Butter Sauce, page 166

Preheat oven to 400F (205C). Generously grease muffin pans. In a medium bowl, combine cranberries and sugar. Let stand a few minutes. Put MUFFIN MIX in a medium bowl. Combine sour cream, egg and butter or margarine or oil with cranberry mixture. Blend well. Add mixture all at once to MUFFIN MIX. Stir until just moistened; batter should be lumpy. Fill prepared muffin pans 3/4 full. Bake 18 to 20 minutes, until golden brown. Serve with warm Hot Butter Sauce. Makes about 10 cakes.

Applesauce Snack Cake

This cake is even better the next day.

1 pkg. SNACK CAKE MIX,
　　page 14
1 egg
1/3 cup vegetable oil
3/4 cup applesauce
1-1/2 teaspoons ground
　　cinnamon
1/2 teaspoon ground allspice
1/8 teaspoon ground cloves
1/2 cup chopped nuts
1 cup raisins

Preheat oven to 325F (165C). Pour SNACK CAKE MIX into ungreased 8- or 9-inch square baking pan; set aside. In a small bowl, combine egg, oil, applesauce, cinnamon, allspice and cloves, beating with a fork to blend. Stir into SNACK CAKE MIX until smooth and blended. Stir in nuts and raisins. Bake 35 to 45 minutes until a wooden pick inserted in center comes out clean. Cool on a rack. Makes 6 servings.

Banana-Walnut Snack Cake

Place a paper doily on the hot cake, dust with powdered sugar, then remove the doily.

1 pkg. SNACK CAKE MIX,
    page 14
1 egg
1/3 cup vegetable oil
1/2 cup mashed ripe banana
1/2 cup buttermilk, milk or
    water
1/2 cup chopped walnuts

Preheat oven to 350F (175C). Pour SNACK CAKE MIX into ungreased 8- or 9-inch square baking pan. In a small bowl, combine remaining ingredients, beating with a fork to blend. Stir into SNACK CAKE MIX until blended. Bake 35 to 45 minutes in preheated oven until a wooden pick inserted in center comes out clean. Cool on a rack. Makes 9 servings.

Carrot Snack Cake

Substitute a 7-ounce jar of junior baby food carrots for the grated carrots and orange juice.

1 pkg. SNACK CAKE MIX,
    page 14
1 egg
1/3 cup vegetable oil
1 cup grated carrots
3/4 cup orange juice
1 teaspoon ground cinnamon
1/2 cup chopped nuts
Cream Cheese Frosting, see
    below

Cream Cheese Frosting:
3 tablespoons butter or
    margarine, softened
1 (3-oz.) pkg. cream cheese,
    softened
1-2/3 cups powdered sugar,
    sifted
1/2 teaspoon vanilla extract

Preheat oven to 350F (175C). Pour SNACK CAKE MIX into an ungreased 8- or 9-inch square baking pan. In a medium bowl, combine egg, oil, carrots, orange juice and cinnamon, beating with a fork to blend. Stir into SNACK CAKE MIX until blended. Stir in nuts. Bake 35 to 45 minutes until a wooden pick inserted in center comes out clean. Prepare frosting; set aside. Cool cake on a rack. Spread frosting evenly over cooled cake. Makes 9 servings.

Cream Cheese Frosting

In a small bowl, cream butter or margarine and cream cheese until light and fluffy. Beat in powdered sugar and vanilla until smooth.

Date-Chocolate Chip Snack Cake

A terrific picnic cake; take it right in the pan.

1/2 cup chopped dates
3/4 cup boiling water
1 pkg. SNACK CAKE MIX,
    page 14
1/2 teaspoon ground cinnamon
1/3 cup vegetable oil
1 egg
1/2 teaspoon vanilla extract
1/2 cup brown sugar, firmly
    packed
1/2 cup chopped nuts
1/2 cup chocolate chips

Preheat oven to 350F (175C). In a small bowl, combine dates and boiling water. Set aside; pour SNACK CAKE MIX into an ungreased 8- or 9-inch square baking pan. Add cinnamon, vegetable oil, egg, vanilla and cooled date mixture. Stir with a fork until all ingredients are blended. Top with brown sugar, nuts and then chocolate chips. Bake 35 to 45 minutes until done. Cool on rack. Makes 9 servings.

Double Chocolate Snack Cake

This moist, delicious cake frosts itself.

1 pkg. SNACK CAKE MIX,
    page 14
2 tablespoons unsweetened cocoa
    powder
3/4 cup water
1 egg
1/3 cup vegetable oil
1 teaspoon vanilla extract
1/2 cup semisweet chocolate
    chips
1/2 cup chopped nuts

Preheat oven to 350F (175C). In an ungreased 8- or 9-inch square baking pan, combine SNACK CAKE MIX and cocoa powder. In a medium bowl, combine water, egg, oil and vanilla. Beat with a fork to blend. Stir into cocoa mixture until smooth and blended. Sprinkle chocolate chips and nuts evenly over top of batter. Bake 35 to 45 minutes in preheated oven until surface springs back when touched with your fingers. Makes 9 servings.

Variation
Bumpy Road Snack Cake: Omit unsweetened cocoa powder. Substitute buttermilk for water.

Gingerbread Snack Cake

Top this with hot lemon sauce for an old-fashioned treat.

1 pkg. SNACK CAKE MIX,
　　page 14
3/4 cup hot water
1/3 cup molasses
1 egg
1/3 cup vegetable oil
1 teaspoon ground cinnamon
1 teaspoon ground ginger
1/2 teaspoon ground cloves
Hot Lemon Sauce, page 176

Preheat oven to 350F (175C). Pour SNACK CAKE MIX into an ungreased 8- or 9-inch square baking pan; set aside. In a medium bowl, combine hot water, molasses, egg, oil, cinnamon, ginger and cloves. Beat with a fork to blend. Stir into SNACK CAKE MIX until blended. Bake 35 to 45 minutes in preheated oven until a wooden pick inserted in center comes out clean. Prepare Hot Lemon Sauce. Serve over warm gingerbread. Makes 9 servings.

Chocolate Cake

Buttermilk gives it a lighter texture.

3-1/3 cups ALL-PURPOSE
　　CAKE MIX, page 15
1/4 cup brown sugar, firmly
　　packed
3/4 cup unsweetened cocoa
　　powder
1/4 teaspoon baking soda
1-1/2 cups buttermilk
3 eggs
1 teaspoon vanilla extract
1/4 cup butter or margarine,
　　melted

Preheat oven to 350F (175C). Generously grease and lightly flour two 8- or 9-inch round cake pans or one 13" x 9" baking pan. In a large bowl, combine ALL-PURPOSE CAKE MIX, brown sugar, cocoa powder and soda. Mix well. Add buttermilk, eggs, vanilla, butter or margarine. Beat with an electric mixer on high speed for 2 to 3 minutes. Scrape batter from sides of bowl with a rubber spatula. Beat another minute. Pour into prepared pans. Bake 8- or 9-inch round pans 25 to 35 minutes; bake 13" x 9" pan 35 to 40 minutes, until a wooden pick inserted in center comes out clean. Cool on a rack 10 minutes. If desired, invert cakes onto rack, remove pans and frost when completely cool. Makes 1 or 2 cakes.

Oatmeal Spice Cake

The topping makes this cake extra special, but it's good plain too.

3/4 cup rolled oats
1-1/4 cups boiling water
1 pkg. SNACK CAKE MIX,
    page 14
1 egg
1/3 cup vegetable oil
1 teaspoon ground cinnamon
1/2 teaspoon ground nutmeg
1 teaspoon vanilla extract
1/2 cup chopped nuts
1/2 cup raisins
Broiled Coconut Topping, see
    below

Broiled Coconut Topping:
4 tablespoons butter or
    margarine
1/4 cup brown sugar, firmly
    packed
2 tablespoons milk
1/2 teaspoon vanilla extract
1/2 cup shredded coconut
1/2 cup chopped nuts

Preheat oven to 325F (165C). Pour rolled oats into a small bowl. Stir in boiling water; set aside. Pour SNACK CAKE MIX in an ungreased 8- or 9-inch square baking pan; set aside. In a medium bowl, combine egg, oil, cinnamon, nutmeg and vanilla. Beat with a fork to blend. Stir in softened rolled oats mixture. Stir into SNACK CAKE MIX until blended. Stir in nuts and raisins until evenly distributed. Bake 45 minutes in preheated oven until a wooden pick inserted in center comes out clean. Prepare topping. Spread topping evenly over cake as it comes from oven. Turn oven to broil. Place cake in oven 3 inches below broiling element. Broil about 2 minutes until frosting bubbles. Makes 9 servings.

Broiled Coconut Topping

In a small saucepan, melt butter or margarine. Stir in remaining ingredients.

Lemon Pound Cake

May be served plain, glazed with a lemon glaze or dusted with powdered sugar.

5 cups ALL-PURPOSE CAKE
  MIX, page 15
1 (3-1/2-oz.) pkg. instant lemon
  pudding mix
1/2 cup butter or margarine,
  melted
1 cup dairy sour cream
1 teaspoon lemon extract
4 eggs

Preheat oven to 350F (175C). Generously grease and lightly flour one 12-cup bundt pan; set aside. In a large bowl, combine ALL-PURPOSE CAKE MIX, pudding mix, butter or margarine, sour cream and lemon extract. Beat with electric mixer on high speed 1 minute. Scrape batter from side of bowl with a rubber spatula. Beat on high speed 1 minute longer. Add eggs 1 at a time, beating well after each addition until batter is creamy. Batter will be thick. Pour into prepared pan. Bake 60 to 70 minutes until a wooden pick inserted in center comes out clean. Cool on a rack 10 minutes. Invert onto rack and remove pan. Makes 12 to 16 servings.

Variation
Almond Poppy Seed Pound Cake: Substitute vanilla instant pudding mix for the lemon pudding mix. Substitute almond extract for the lemon extract. Add 1/4 cup poppy seeds.

Yellow Cake

The secret to this moist, tender cake is to beat the batter until creamy.

5 cups ALL-PURPOSE CAKE
    MIX, page 15
1-1/4 cups milk
1 teaspoon vanilla extract
3 eggs

Preheat oven to 350F (175C). Generously grease and lightly flour two 8- or 9-inch round cake pans or one 13" x 9" baking pan; set aside. In a large bowl, combine ALL-PURPOSE CAKE MIX, milk and vanilla. Beat with electric mixer on high speed 1 minute. Scrape batter from side of bowl with a rubber spatula. Beat on high 1 minute longer. Add eggs 1 at a time beating well after each addition until batter is creamy. Pour into prepared pans. Bake 30 to 35 minutes for 8- or 9-inch round pans; bake 13" x 9" pan 35 to 40 minutes, until a wooden pick inserted in center comes out clean. Cool on a rack 10 minutes. Invert onto rack and remove pan, if desired. Frost, if desired, when cake is completely cool. Makes 1 or 2 cakes.

Variation

White Cake: Use only egg whites.

Small Cake: Use half the ingredients (using 2 egg yolks or whites) and bake in 8-inch square pan.

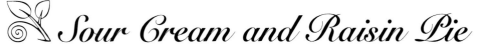

Sour Cream and Raisin Pie

To change the pie, top it with Mile-High Meringue from Sour Cream and Lemon Pie, page 169.

Single Freezer Pie Crust, baked,
    page 33
2/3 cup VANILLA PUDDING
    AND PIE FILLING MIX,
    page 16
2-1/2 cups milk
1/4 teaspoon ground nutmeg
1/4 teaspoon ground cinnamon
1/3 cup raisins
2 tablespoons butter or
    margarine
1 teaspoon vanilla extract
1 cup dairy sour cream
2 cups sweetened whipped cream

Prepare pie crust in a 9-inch pie plate; set aside to cool. In a medium saucepan, combine VANILLA PUDDING AND PIE FILLING MIX, milk, nutmeg, cinnamon and raisins. Cook and stir over medium heat until mixture thickens and begins to bubble, 3 to 5 minutes. Remove from heat. Stir in butter or margarine and vanilla until blended. Cover with plastic wrap. Cool on a rack. Fold in sour cream. Pour into baked pie crust. Refrigerate about 2 hours. Top with sweetened whipped cream. Makes about 8 servings.

 Vanilla Cream Pie

This creamy pie filling has no eggs in it.

Single Freezer Pie Crust, baked, page 33
2/3 cup VANILLA PUDDING AND PIE FILLING MIX, page 16
2-1/2 cups milk
2 tablespoons butter or margarine
1-1/2 teaspoon vanilla extract

Prepare crust in a 9-inch pie plate; set aside to cool. In a medium saucepan, combine VANILLA PUDDING AND PIE FILLING MIX and milk. Cook and stir over medium heat until mixture thickens and begins to bubble, 3 to 5 minutes. Remove from heat. Stir in butter or margarine and vanilla until blended. Cover with plastic wrap. Cool on a rack. Pour into baked pie crust. Refrigerate about 2 hours. Makes about 8 servings.

Variations
Banana Cream Pie: Slice 2 ripe bananas into pie crust before adding filling.

Strawberry Cream Pie: Stir 2 to 4 tablespoons sugar into 2 cups sliced strawberries. Let stand 1 hour. Drain off juice. Spoon sweetened strawberries into baked pie crust. Pour chilled filling over strawberries. Top with 2 cups sweetened whipped cream.

Coconut Cream Pie: Fold 3/4 cup shredded coconut into cooled filling. Garnish with sweetened whipped cream and 1/4 cup toasted shredded coconut.

Mom's Spumoni Cake

This prize winner is a delightful blend of flavors and colors.

Rainbow Frosting, see below
3-1/3 cups ALL-PURPOSE
  CAKE MIX, page 15
1/4 cup brown sugar, firmly
  packed
3/4 cup unsweetened cocoa
  powder
1/4 teaspoon baking soda
1-1/2 cups buttermilk
3 eggs
1 teaspoon vanilla extract
1/4 cup butter or margarine,
  melted

Rainbow Frosting:

1 cup milk
2 tablespoons all-purpose flour
Pinch of salt
1/2 cup butter or margarine,
  softened
1/2 cup vegetable shortening
1 cup granulated sugar
2 to 3 drops green food coloring
1/4 teaspoon almond flavoring
2 to 3 drops yellow food coloring
1/4 teaspoon lemon flavoring
2 to 3 drops red food coloring
1/4 teaspoon peppermint
  flavoring
3 tablespoons unsweetened cocoa
  powder
1/4 teaspoon vanilla extract

Prepare Rainbow Frosting and set aside. Preheat oven to 350F (175C). Generously grease and lightly flour two 8- or 9-inch round cake pans. In a large bowl, combine ALL-PURPOSE CAKE MIX, brown sugar, cocoa powder and soda. Mix well. Add buttermilk, eggs, vanilla and butter or margarine. Beat with electric mixer on high speed for 2 to 3 minutes. Scrape batter from sides of bowl with a rubber spatula. Beat another minute. Pour into prepared pans. Bake 25 to 35 minutes, until a wooden pick inserted in center comes out clean. Cool on a rack 10 minutes. When completely cool, cut each cake with a serrated knife to make 2 layers each. Frost each layer with a different color of Rainbow Frosting. Stack layers. Do not frost sides. Makes one 4-layer cake.

Rainbow Frosting

In a small saucepan, combine milk, flour and salt. Cook over medium heat about 5 to 7 minutes, until thickened. Cool. Combine butter or margarine, shortening and sugar in a medium bowl. Beat well. Add to cooled milk mixture, beating constantly. Beat about 7 minutes, until smooth. Divide mixture among 4 bowls. In the first bowl, add green food coloring and almond flavoring. In the second bowl, add yellow food coloring and lemon flavoring. In a third bowl, add red food coloring and peppermint flavoring. Add cocoa powder and vanilla to the fourth bowl.

Mom's Spumoni Cake

Chocolate Cream Pie

Make Chocolate Banana Cream Pie by slicing 2 bananas into the baked pie crust.

Single Freezer Pie Crust, baked, page 33
1 cup CHOCOLATE PUDDING AND PIE FILLING MIX, page 16
2-1/2 cups milk
2 tablespoons butter or margarine
1 teaspoon vanilla extract
2 cups sweetened whipped cream, if desired

Prepare pie crust in a 9-inch pie plate; set aside to cool. In a medium saucepan, combine CHOCOLATE PUDDING AND PIE FILLING MIX and milk. Cook and stir over medium heat until mixture thickens and begins to bubble, 3 to 5 minutes. Cook and stir 1 minute longer. Remove from heat. Stir in butter or margarine and vanilla until blended. Cool slightly. Pour into pie crust; cover with plastic wrap. Refrigerate 2 to 3 hours. To serve, top with sweetened whipped cream, if desired. Makes about 8 servings.

Luscious Lemon Pie

Tart and well worth the pucker!

Single Freezer Pie Crust, baked, page 33
1-1/4 cups LEMON PIE FILLING MIX, page 17
2-1/2 cups water
3 egg yolks
2 tablespoons butter or margarine
Sweetened whipped cream

Prepare pie crust. In a large saucepan, combine LEMON PIE FILLING MIX, 1/2 cup of the water and egg yolks. Mix until smooth. Add remaining 2 cups water. Cook over medium heat, about 4 to 5 minutes, stirring constantly until mixture is thick and bubbly. Remove from heat. Add butter or margarine. Stir until melted. Cover and let cool 5 minutes. Stir. Pour into baked pie crust. Cover and refrigerate 3 hours. Top with whipped cream before serving. Makes one 9-inch single-crust pie.

Variation
Meringue Topping: Omit whipped cream topping. In a deep metal or glass bowl, beat 3 egg whites until stiff, gradually adding 6 tablespoons sugar. Spread on top of warm pie, sealing to edges. Preheat oven to 400F (205C). Bake 8 to 10 minutes, until meringue is lightly browned. Cool pie on a wire rack, then refrigerate.

Texas Sheet Cake

A Bi-i-i-i-g Brownie Cake!

4 cups BROWNIE MIX, page 19
1/2 cup butter or margarine
1 cup water
1/2 cup dairy sour cream
2 eggs, slightly beaten
1 teaspoon baking soda
Cocoa Icing, see below

Cocoa Icing:
1/2 cup evaporated milk
1/2 cup butter or margarine
3 tablespoons unsweetened cocoa
   powder
3 cups powdered sugar
1 cup chopped nuts
1 teaspoon vanilla extract

Preheat oven to 375F (190C). Grease a 15" x 10" or larger baking pan. Put BROWNIE MIX in a large bowl. In a small saucepan, bring butter or margarine and water to a boil. Add to BROWNIE MIX. Add sour cream, eggs and baking soda. Blend well. Pour into prepared pan. Bake 20 to 25 minutes, until a toothpick inserted in center comes out clean. Prepare Cocoa Icing. Frost cake while still hot. Makes one large cake.

Cocoa Icing

In a small saucepan, bring evaporated milk, butter or margarine and cocoa to a boil, stirring constantly. Remove from heat. Add to powdered sugar in a medium bowl. Stir in nuts and vanilla.

Fresh Peach Pie

When they are in season, use fresh strawberries instead of peaches.

Single Freezer Pie Crust, baked,
   page 33
1 cup fresh peaches, crushed
1/3 cup water
1 cup sugar
4 tablespoons cornstarch
Pinch salt
1/4 cup water
1 tablespoon lemon juice
1 tablespoon butter or
   margarine
3 to 4 cups sliced fresh peaches
2 cups sweetened whipped
   cream, for garnish

Prepare pie crust in a 9-inch pie plate; set aside to cool. In a medium saucepan, combine 1 cup crushed peaches and 1/3 cup water. Stir constantly over medium heat until mixture begins to boil. Cook and stir about 2 minutes longer. Remove from heat. In a medium bowl, combine sugar, cornstarch, salt, 1/4 cup water and lemon juice, beating with a wire whisk to blend. Stir into cooked peach mixture. Cook and stir over medium heat until slightly thickened. Stir in butter or margarine until blended. Set aside to cool. Arrange 3 to 4 cups sliced peaches in prepared pie crust. Spoon cooled mixture over peaches. Refrigerate 2 hours. To serve, cut in wedges. Garnish each wedge with a dollop of sweetened whipped cream. Makes about 8 servings.

Cherry-Almond Pie

For special occasions, make a lattice-top crust by weaving strips of dough.

2 (1-lb.) cans pitted tart red
    cherries
1-1/4 cups sugar
1/3 cup all-purpose flour
1/4 teaspoon salt
1 tablespoon butter or
    margarine, melted
1/4 teaspoon almond extract
1/4 teaspoon red food coloring, if
    desired
Double Freezer Pie Crust,
    unbaked, page 33
Almond Glaze, see below

Almond Glaze:
1 cup powdered sugar
1/2 teaspoon almond extract
About 2 tablespoons cream or
    milk

Drain cherries, reserving 1/2 cup juice. In a medium bowl, combine cherries, sugar, flour, salt, butter or margarine, almond extract, 1/2 cup reserved cherry juice and food coloring, if desired. Let stand about 10 minutes. Preheat oven to 425F (220C). Prepare bottom pie crust in a 9-inch pie plate. Pour cherry mixture into unbaked crust. Cover with top crust. Cut slits in top crust to let steam escape. Trim and flute edges. Bake about 40 minutes in preheated oven until evenly browned. Prepare glaze. Brush top of hot pie with Almond Glaze. Makes about 8 servings.

Almond Glaze

In a small bowl, combine powdered sugar, almond extract and enough cream or milk to make a thin mixture.

All-American Apple Pie

It's exquisite!

1 Double Freezer Pie Crust,
    unbaked, page 33
8 or 9 tart cooking apples,
    pared, cored and sliced thin
Juice of 1 lemon (about 1/4 cup)
6 tablespoons all-purpose flour
3/4 cup sugar, more if desired
1 teaspoon ground cinnamon
1 teaspoon ground nutmeg
2 tablespoons butter

Hot Butter Sauce:
1/2 cup butter
1 cup sugar
1 cup cream, or evaporated milk
Dash of nutmeg

Prepare bottom crust in a 9-inch pie plate. Put apples in a large bowl. Toss with lemon juice. Set aside. Preheat oven to 400F (205C). In a small bowl, combine flour, sugar, cinnamon and nutmeg. Sprinkle about 1/4 cup of mixture on the bottom pie crust and add the rest to the apples. Stir to coat apples. Fill pie crust heaping full of apple mixture. Dot with butter. Place top crust over filling. Press edges together and flute. Cut slits in top crust to let steam escape. Bake about 50 minutes, until crust is golden. Serve with Hot Butter Sauce. Makes one 9-inch double-crust pie.

Hot Butter Sauce

Combine butter, sugar and cream or evaporated milk in a small saucepan. Cook over medium heat about 3 to 5 minutes, until butter melts and sugar is dissolved. Do not boil. Remove from heat. Add nutmeg. Serve warm. Makes about 1-1/4 cups sauce.

All-American Apple Pie with Hot Butter Sauce

Chess Tarts

Serve these Southern favorites at a holiday buffet.

1 pkg. CREAM CHEESE
    PASTRY MIX, page 34,
    thawed
1/2 cup butter or margarine,
    softened
1-1/4 cups sugar
3 eggs, separated
3/4 cup raisins
3/4 cup chopped nuts
1 teaspoon vanilla extract

Divide CREAM CHEESE PASTRY MIX into 10 pieces. Shape each piece into a ball. Place each ball in a medium muffin cup. Use your thumbs to press dough over bottom and up side of each cup, keeping dough at an even thickness; set aside. In a large bowl, cream butter or margarine and sugar. Add egg yolks 1 at a time, beating thoroughly after each addition. Stir in raisins, nuts and vanilla. Preheat oven to 400F (205C). In a medium bowl, beat egg whites until soft peaks form. Fold into creamed mixture. Fill each pastry shell about 3/4 full with batter. Bake 15 minutes in preheated oven. Reduce temperature to 325F (165C). Bake 10 to 15 minutes longer until golden brown. Makes 10 tarts.

Lime Tarts Supreme

Creamy chiffon filling is topped with a dollop of whipped cream and grated lime peel.

1 pkg. CREAM CHEESE
    PASTRY MIX, page 34,
    thawed
Lime Filling, see below

Lime Filling:
2 eggs
1/2 cup sugar
1/4 cup lime juice
1 teaspoon grated lime peel
1/4 cup butter or margarine
2 drops green food coloring, if
    desired
1 cup whipping cream, whipped

Preheat oven to 400F (205C). Divide CREAM CHEESE PASTRY MIX into 10 pieces. Shape each piece into a ball. Place each ball in a medium muffin cup. Use your thumbs to press dough over the bottom and up side of each cup, keeping dough at an even thickness. Bake in preheated oven 10 minutes or until lightly browned. Cool on a rack. Prepare Lime Filling. Carefully remove cooled tart shells from muffin cups. Spoon filling evenly into shells. Garnish with reserved whipped cream and reserved lime peel from filling. Makes 10 tarts.

Lime Filling

In a small bowl, beat eggs until light and pale. Beat in sugar, lime juice and half of lime peel until blended. Pour into top of double boiler. Add butter or margarine. Cook and stir over hot water until thickened. Remove from heat. Stir in food coloring, if desired. Refrigerate 1 hour. Reserve 3 tablespoons whipped cream. Fold remaining whipped cream into chilled egg mixture.

Pecan Tarts

Miniature pecan pies are always a welcome treat for family or guests.

1 pkg. CREAM CHEESE
  PASTRY MIX, page 34,
  thawed
2 eggs, slightly beaten
2 tablespoons butter or
  margarine, melted
1-1/2 cups brown sugar, firmly
  packed
1/8 teaspoon salt
2 teaspoons vanilla extract
1-1/4 cup chopped pecans

Divide CREAM CHEESE PASTRY MIX into 10 pieces. Shape each piece into a ball. Place each ball in a medium muffin cup. Use your thumbs to press dough over bottom and up side of each cup, keeping dough at an even thickness; set aside. In a large bowl, combine eggs, butter or margarine, brown sugar, salt and vanilla, beating with a wire whisk until blended. Stir in pecans. Preheat oven to 325F (165C). Fill each pastry shell about 3/4 full. Bake 25 minutes in preheated oven until golden brown. Makes 10 tarts.

Sour Cream and Lemon Pie

This meringue won't stick to your fork as you eat it.

Single Freezer Pie Crust, baked,
  page 33
1 cup sugar
5 tablespoons cornstarch
Pinch salt
1 cup milk
3 egg yolks
4 tablespoons butter or
  margarine
1 teaspoon grated lemon peel
1/3 cup fresh lemon juice
1 cup dairy sour cream
Mile-High Meringue, see below

Mile-High Meringue:
1 tablespoon cornstarch
3 tablespoons sugar
Pinch salt
1 teaspoon lemon juice
1/2 cup water
3 egg whites, room temperature
6 tablespoons sugar

Prepare pie crust in a 9-inch pie plate; set aside to cool. In a small saucepan, combine sugar, cornstarch and salt. Gradually stir in milk. Cook and stir over medium heat until smooth and slightly thickened; set aside. In a small bowl, beat egg yolks with a wire whisk. Beating vigorously, add about half of hot mixture. Slowly stir egg mixture into remaining hot mixture. Cook and stir 2 minutes; set aside. Stir in butter or margarine, lemon peel and lemon juice. Cover with plastic wrap. Cool on a rack. Fold in sour cream. Pour into prepared pie crust; set aside. Prepare Mile-High Meringue. Preheat oven to 325F (165C). Spoon meringue on top of pie, spreading to seal completely. Bake 20 to 30 minutes in preheated oven until golden brown. Makes about 8 servings.

Mile-High Meringue

In a small saucepan, combine cornstarch, 3 tablespoons sugar, salt, lemon juice and water. Cook and stir over medium heat until clear and thickened. Set aside to cool. In a large bowl, beat egg whites until soft peaks form. Gradually add cooled cornstarch mixture, beating until mixture thickens. Gradually add 6 tablespoons sugar, beating until soft peaks form, 5 to 8 minutes.

Desserts and More

Be a "Supermom" by filling your home with the tempting aroma of freshly baked cookies. They speak a language that says "welcome." In this chapter, you'll find chewy cookies, bar cookies and many others. Also see *Special Mixes* for our selection of SLICE AND BAKE COOKIES.

If you're looking for a way to introduce cookies to your children, BASIC COOKIE MIX is made to order. They'll hardly have a chance to make a mess! Successes right from the beginning will motivate them to move on to more challenging mixes.

Children might have the right idea when they eat main dishes sparingly to save room for the finishing touch—dessert! A meal without a dessert is like a kitchen without a sink. Many desserts add nutrition to a meal, such as puddings or fruit-filled desserts.

When planning your menus, include desserts that will complement the meal. For example, serve a light dessert such as Lemonade Ice Cream Dessert when you have a meal of pasta or other substantial food. Save your rich desserts like Banana Split Cake or Blueberry Dessert for lighter meals.

Need a spectacular dessert for a special occasion? Try the Cookie Crust Fruit Tart. In addition to being beautiful, it's delicious and easy. Check the Cakes and Pies section for other great finales.

Mini-Peanut Butter and Chocolate Cookies

This favorite peanut butter-chocolate candy makes these cookies a hit at a dessert buffet.

1 roll SLICE AND BAKE
    PEANUT BUTTER
    COOKIES, page 48, thawed
    slightly
1 (9-oz.) pkg. miniature peanut
    butter cups

Preheat oven to 350F (175C). Cut dough into 1-inch-thick slices. Cut each slice into fourths. Place dough into mini-muffin pans. Bake 8 to 10 minutes, until lightly browned around the edges. While cookies are baking, unwrap miniature peanut butter cups. Remove baked cookies from the oven and press a miniature peanut butter cup into the center of each baked cookie. Cool slightly. Refrigerate for 30 minutes before removing from muffin pans. Makes 36 cookies.

Cookie Crust Fruit Tart

To make individual tarts, roll out dough, cut and bake as if making cookies. Cool and proceed as described below.

1 roll SLICE AND BAKE
    SUGAR COOKIES, page 46,
    thawed
Cream Cheese Filling, see below
Glaze, see below
2 to 3 cups fresh or canned
    fruits, drained (strawberries,
    kiwi, bananas, grapes,
    mandarin oranges, pineapple)

Cream Cheese Filling:
1 (8-oz.) pkg. cream cheese,
    softened
1/2 cup granulated sugar
1 teaspoon vanilla extract

Glaze:
1 tablespoon cornstarch
1/2 cup orange juice
1/4 cup water
2 tablespoons sugar
2 tablespoons fresh lemon juice

Preheat oven to 350F (175C). Press thawed cookie dough onto a 12-inch quiche pan with removable bottom or a 12-inch pizza pan to a thickness of about 1/4 inch. Make rim around edge of cookie. Bake for 15 to 20 minutes or until lightly browned around edges. Cool. Prepare Cream Cheese Filling. Spread on top of cookie to within 1/2 inch of edge. Prepare Glaze; set aside to cool. Decorate cookie in concentric circles with assorted fresh and canned fruits. Brush top of fruit with Glaze. Cover with plastic wrap and chill until served. To serve, cut into wedges. Makes 8 to 12 servings.

Cream Cheese Filling

In a small bowl, combine all ingredients until smooth.

Glaze

In a small saucepan, combine all ingredients and bring to a boil. Boil 1 minute. Cool.

Molasses Cookies

Soft and chewy.

2 cups QUICK MIX, page 11
1/4 cup sugar
1/2 teaspoon ground cinnamon
1/2 teaspoon ground ginger
1/4 teaspoon ground cloves
1 egg yolk
1/2 cup molasses
Sugar

In a medium bowl, combine QUICK MIX, 1/4 cup sugar, cinnamon, ginger and cloves. Mix well. Combine egg yolk and molasses in a small bowl. Add to dry mixture. Blend well. Refrigerate at least one hour. Preheat oven to 375F (190C). Lightly grease baking sheets. Shape dough into 1-1/2-inch balls, and roll in sugar. Place on prepared baking sheets. Flatten balls with the bottom of a glass dipped in sugar. Bake 8 to 10 minutes, until edges are browned. Makes about 30 cookies.

Caramel-Nut Pudding Cake

Delicate cake and scrumptious caramel pudding—what a combination!

1 cup QUICK MIX, page 11
1/2 cup brown sugar, firmly packed
1/2 cup raisins, if desired
1/2 cup chopped nuts
1/2 cup milk
Brown Sugar Topping, see below

Brown Sugar Topping:
1 cup brown sugar, firmly packed
1 tablespoon butter or margarine
2 cups boiling water

Preheat oven to 375F (190C). Lightly grease an 8-inch square pan. In a medium bowl, combine QUICK MIX, brown sugar, raisins, if desired, and nuts. Mix well. Add milk and blend well. Pour into prepared pan. Prepare Brown Sugar Topping. Gently pour over top of cake mixture without stirring. Bake 30 to 40 minutes, until cake springs back when lightly touched in center. Cool in pan 15 minutes before serving. Makes one 8-inch cake.

Brown Sugar Topping

In a small bowl, combine brown sugar, butter or margarine and boiling water. Blend.

Hot Fudge Pudding Cake

Chocolate cake on top and a fudgy pudding sauce below. Serve it á la mode!

1-1/2 cups QUICK MIX, page 11
1/2 cup granulated sugar
2 tablespoons cocoa
3/4 cup chopped nuts
1/2 cup milk
1 teaspoon vanilla extract
3/4 cup brown sugar, firmly
    packed
1/4 cup cocoa
1-1/2 cups boiling water

Preheat oven to 350F (175C). In an unbuttered, 8-inch square pan, combine QUICK MIX, granulated sugar, 2 tablespoons cocoa, nuts, milk and vanilla. Blend well. Combine brown sugar and 1/4 cup cocoa in a small bowl. Sprinkle over top of cake mixture. Gently pour boiling water over top of mixture. Do not stir. Bake 35 to 40 minutes, until edges separate from pan. Cool in pan 15 minutes before serving. Makes one 8-inch cake.

Variation
Omit nuts and add 1 cup miniature marshmallows.

Sunday Shortcake

The old-fashioned way, with your choice of fruit.

3 cups QUICK MIX, page 11
2 tablespoons sugar
1/4 cup butter or margarine,
    melted
1/2 cup milk or water
1 egg, well-beaten
Fruit, as desired
Whipped cream

Preheat oven to 400F (205C). Combine QUICK MIX and sugar in a medium bowl. Mix well. In a small bowl, combine melted butter or margarine, milk or water and egg. Add to dry ingredients. Stir with a fork until just moistened. On a lightly floured surface, knead 8 to 10 times. Roll out dough to 1/2-inch thickness. Cut with a lightly floured 3-inch, round cutter. Bake on an unbuttered baking sheet about 10 minutes, until golden brown. Cool. Top with fruit as desired and whipped cream. Makes 6 shortcakes.

Boston Cream Pie

In a hurry? Use one-half recipe Yellow Cake, page 160, for the cake base.

1-1/4 cups sifted cake flour
3/4 cup sugar
1-1/2 teaspoons baking powder
1/2 teaspoon salt
1/4 cup butter or margarine,
    softened
1/2 cup milk
1 teaspoon vanilla extract
2 tablespoons milk
1 egg
Cream Filling, see below
Chocolate Frosting, see below

Cream Filling:
1 egg yolk
1/3 cup VANILLA PUDDING
    AND PIE FILLING MIX,
    page 16
1-1/4 cups milk
1 tablespoon butter or
    margarine
1 teaspoon vanilla extract

Chocolate Frosting:
1 cup sifted powdered sugar
2 tablespoons hot water
1 (1-oz.) square unsweetened
    chocolate, melted
1 teaspoon butter or margarine,
    melted

Preheat oven to 350F (175C). Grease and flour an 8-inch, round cake pan or a 6-inch square baking pan. In a medium bowl, combine cake flour, sugar, baking powder and salt. Stir in softened butter or margarine and 1/2 cup milk. Beat 2 minutes with an electric mixer or 5 minutes by hand. Stir in vanilla, 2 tablespoons milk and egg. Beat 2 minutes longer. Pour batter into prepared pan. Bake 30 minutes until cake is lightly browned and a wooden pick inserted in center comes out clean. Cool on a rack. Use a knife with a long thin blade to cut cake in half horizontally. Prepare Cream Filling; let cool. Prepare Chocolate Frosting; set aside. Place bottom layer of split cake on a 10-inch, round platter. Spread cooled filling evenly over bottom cake layer. Gently place top layer of split cake on top of filling. Spread frosting over top layer. Refrigerate 3 to 4 hours. Makes 8 servings.

Cream Filling

In a small bowl, lightly beat egg yolk; set aside. In a small saucepan, combine VANILLA PUDDING AND PIE FILLLING MIX and milk. Cook and stir over medium heat until mixture thickens and begins to bubble, 3 to 5 minutes. Stirring vigorously, pour about half of hot milk mixture into beaten egg yolk. Slowly stir egg mixture into remaining hot milk mixture. Cook and stir l minute longer. Remove from heat. Stir in butter or margarine and vanilla until blended. Cover with plastic wrap; cool on a rack.

Chocolate Frosting

In a medium bowl, combine powdered sugar and water. Beat in chocolate and butter or margarine until smooth.

Creamy Vanilla Pudding

Omit the egg yolks if you prefer a lighter pudding.

2 egg yolks
2/3 cup VANILLA PUDDING
 AND PIE FILLING MIX,
 page 16
2-3/4 cups milk
2 tablespoons butter or
 margarine
1-1/2 teaspoons vanilla extract

In a medium bowl, beat egg yolks; set aside. In a medium saucepan, combine VANILLA PUDDING AND PIE FILLING MIX and milk. Cook and stir over medium heat until mixture thickens and begins to bubble. Stirring vigorously, pour about half of the hot mixture into beaten egg yolks. Stir egg yolk mixture into remaining hot mixture. Cook and stir 1 minute longer. Remove from heat. Stir in butter or margarine and vanilla until blended. Pour cooked pudding into 6 dessert or custard cups. Cover each with plastic wrap. Refrigerate 1 hour. Makes 6 servings.

Variation
Creamy Chocolate Pudding: Omit egg yolks. Substitute 1 cup CHOCOLATE PUDDING AND PIE FILLING MIX, page 16, for VANILLA PUDDING AND PIE FILLING MIX.

Layered Chocolate and Vanilla Dessert

You can also use Graham Cracker Pie Crust, page 21, with this dessert.

1 cup butter or margarine
1 cup finely chopped nuts
1 cup all-purpose flour
1 cup powdered sugar
1 (8-oz.) pkg. cream cheese,
 softened
1 cup whipping cream, whipped
Creamy Chocolate Pudding,
 page 175, chilled
Creamy Vanilla Pudding, page
 175, chilled
2 cups sweetened whipped
 cream, if desired
1/2 cup shredded coconut, if
 desired

Preheat oven to 325F (165C). In a medium bowl, combine butter or margarine, nuts and flour until crumbly. Press into bottom of a 13" x 9" baking pan. Bake for 25 to 30 minutes in preheated oven until lightly browned. Cool on a rack. In a medium bowl, combine powdered sugar and cream cheese, beating until smooth. Fold in whipped cream. Carefully pour over prepared crust. Spread chocolate pudding evenly over cream cheese mixture and vanilla pudding over chocolate pudding. Garnish with sweetened whipped cream and coconut, if desired. Makes about 15 servings.

Layered Vanilla Cream

You'll like this French-style dessert as much as we do.

1-1/4 cups VANILLA
   PUDDING AND PIE
   FILLING MIX, page 16
3-2/3 cups milk
3 tablespoons butter or
   margarine
1-1/2 teaspoons vanilla extract
Chocolate Glaze Topping, see
   below
1 cup whipping cream
45 single graham crackers (do
   not crush)

Chocolate Glaze Topping:
2 (1-oz.) squares semisweet
   chocolate
6 tablespoons butter or
   margarine
2 tablespoons white corn syrup
2 teaspoons vanilla extract
1-1/2 cups powdered sugar
3 tablespoons milk

In a medium saucepan, combine VANILLA PUDDING AND PIE FILLING MIX and milk. Cook and stir over medium heat until mixture begins to bubble, 3 to 5 minutes. Remove from heat. Stir in butter or margarine and vanilla until blended. Cover with plastic wrap. Cool on a rack. Prepare topping; set aside. In a large bowl, whip cream until stiff peaks form. Fold into cooled pudding mixture. Arrange 15 single graham crackers in bottom of a 13" x 9" baking dish. Spread half of pudding mixture over crackers. Repeat layers. Arrange remaining 15 single graham crackers on top. Pour Chocolate Glaze Topping over top layer of crackers. Cover with plastic wrap. Refrigerate at least 10 hours. Makes 12 servings.

Chocolate Glaze Topping

In a small saucepan, melt chocolate and butter or margarine. Stir in corn syrup, vanilla, powdered sugar and milk, beating until smooth.

Hot Lemon Sauce

Great over warm gingerbread or steamed pudding.

1 cup water
1/4 cup LEMON PIE FILLING
   MIX, page 17
2 tablespoons butter or
   margarine

Combine water and LEMON PIE FILLING MIX in a small saucepan. Bring to a boil over high heat, stirring constantly. Remove from heat. Add butter or margarine and stir to melt. Serve warm over gingerbread, pound cake, apple pie, steamed pudding or other desserts.

Chocolate Filled Pirouette Cookies

Dip one end of each filled cookie in melted chocolate, then in finely chopped nuts.

Chocolate Cream Pie filling,
  page 164, cooled
2 (5-1/2-oz.) boxes pirouette
  cookies

Spoon cooled filling into a pastry tube with a small round tip. Using gentle pressure, squeeze mixture evenly into each cookie. Return cookies to original box. Wrap box in foil; refrigerate at least 1 hour or freeze up to 1 month. Makes 48 filled cookies.

Variations
Vanilla Filled Pirouette Cookies: Substitute Vanilla Cream Pie filling, page 161, for Chocolate Cream Pie filling.

Black and White Pirouette Cookies: Combine 1/2 cup whipping cream, whipped, 1 (3-oz.) package softened cream cheese and 2 tablespoons powdered sugar. Fill half of each cookie with cream cheese mixture. Complete filling cookies with Chocolate Cream Pie filling.

Chewy Chocolate Cookies

Crown each one with a nut.

2 eggs, slightly beaten
1/4 cup water
2-1/4 cups BROWNIE MIX,
  page 19
1/2 teaspoon baking soda
3/4 cup all-purpose flour
1 teaspoon vanilla extract
Walnut or pecan halves

Preheat oven to 375F (190C). Grease baking sheets. Combine eggs and water in a medium bowl. Beat with a fork until blended. Stir in BROWNIE MIX, baking soda, flour and vanilla. Blend well. Drop by teaspoonfuls 2 inches apart on prepared baking sheets. Put a walnut or pecan half in center of each cookie. Bake 10 to 12 minutes, until edges are browned. Cool on wire racks. Makes about 36 cookies.

Our Best Brownies

A delightful, chewy treat.

2 eggs, beaten
1 teaspoon vanilla extract
2-1/2 cups BROWNIE MIX,
    page 19
1/2 cup chopped nuts
Brownie Toppers, see below

Preheat oven to 350F (175C). Grease and flour an 8-inch square pan. In a medium bowl, combine eggs, vanilla and BROWNIE MIX. Beat until smooth. Stir in nuts. Pour into prepared pan. Bake 30 to 35 minutes, until edges separate from pan. Cool. Cut into 2-inch bars. Sprinkle or frost with Brownie Topper of your choice. Makes 16 brownies.

Variation
For cake-like brownies, add 2 tablespoons milk to batter.

Brownie Toppers

Powdered Sugar Sprinkle: Sprinkle warm brownies with powdered sugar.

Chocolate Topper: Sprinkle contents of 1 (6-oz.) package chocolate chips over warm brownies. Warm in oven until melted. Spread evenly on brownies. Sprinkle with chopped nuts, if desired.

Chocolate Mint Topper: Spread contents of 1 (5-1/2-oz.) package chocolate-covered mints over warm brownies. Warm in oven until melted. Spread evenly on brownies.

Marshmallow Surprise: Prepare 1/2 recipe Chocolate Icing, page 180. Sprinkle 1-1/2 cups miniature marshmallows over warm brownies. Warm in oven until melted, about 2 to 3 minutes. Frost with Cocoa Icing.

Bittersweet Frosting: In a small saucepan, combine 1-1/2 cups powdered sugar, 1/2 cup butter or margarine and 1/2 cup evaporated milk. Cook over medium-high heat about 7 to 10 minutes, until temperature reaches 230F (110C). Cool mixture. Beat until stiff and spread on brownies. In a small saucepan, melt 2 (1-oz.) squares unsweetened chocolate over low heat, and spread over topping.

Coconut-Pecan Topping: In a small saucepan, combine 1/3 cup sugar, 1/3 cup evaporated milk, 1 beaten egg yolk and 3 tablespoons butter or margarine. Cook over medium heat about 5 minutes, stirring constantly, until mixture comes to a boil. Remove from heat and stir in 1/4 teaspoon vanilla, 2/3 cup flaked coconut and 1/2 cup chopped pecans. Cool 10 minutes. Spread on cooled brownies.

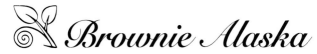

Brownie Alaska

Prepare it ahead of time for a spectacular, but simple dessert.

1 quart vanilla ice cream,
    softened slightly
2 cups BROWNIE MIX, page 19
4 eggs, separated
2 tablespoons water
1 teaspoon vanilla extract
1/2 cup coarsely chopped
    walnuts
1/2 cup sugar

Line a medium bowl with aluminum foil. Pack ice cream into bowl and freeze until very firm. Preheat oven to 350F (175C). Grease an 8-inch, round cake pan. Line pan with wax paper. Grease wax paper. In another medium bowl, combine BROWNIE MIX, egg yolks, water, vanilla and nuts. Spread in prepared pan. Bake about 25 minutes, until edges separate from pan. Cool in pan 10 minutes, then cool on a wire rack. Carefully peel off wax paper. Place cake in the center of a wooden cutting board or a baking sheet lined with heavy brown paper. Cover with plastic wrap. Chill in freezer about 1 hour until hard. In a glass or metal bowl, beat egg whites until foamy. Gradually add sugar and beat until stiff peaks form. Set aside. Quickly invert bowl of ice cream over cake. Lift off bowl and remove foil. Quickly spread meringue evenly over ice cream and brownie, sealing meringue to cutting board or paper. Return to freezer at least 30 minutes. Just before serving, preheat oven to 500F (260C). Bake about 3 minutes, until meringue is lightly browned. Cut in wedges with a knife dipped in warm water. Refreeze leftover Brownie Alaska, if desired. Makes 10 to 12 servings.

Variation
Substitute mint chocolate chip or peppermint ice cream for vanilla ice cream.

Snickerdoodles

Soft when they're warm and snappy when they're cool!

2-1/2 cups BASIC COOKIE
    MIX, page 19
1/4 teaspoon baking soda
1 teaspoon cream of tartar
1 egg
2 tablespoons sugar
1 teaspoon ground cinnamon

Preheat oven to 400F (205C). In a medium bowl, combine BASIC COOKIE MIX, baking soda, cream of tartar and egg. Mix well. Combine sugar and cinnamon in a small dish. Shape dough into 1-1/2-inch balls. Roll in sugar-cinnamon mixture and place 2 inches apart on unbuttered baking sheets. Flatten balls slightly. Bake 8 to 10 minutes, until lightly browned with cracked tops. Makes about 24 cookies.

Mississippi Mud

Appropriately named for its appearance—and incredibly delicious!

4 eggs
1/2 cup butter or margarine, melted
3 cups BROWNIE MIX, page 19
1 teaspoon vanilla extract
2 cups chopped nuts
1 cup flaked coconut
1 (7-oz.) jar marshmallow creme
Chocolate Icing, see below

Chocolate Icing:
1 lb. powdered sugar
1/2 cup butter or margarine
6 tablespoons evaporated milk
4 tablespoons unsweetened cocoa powder

Preheat oven to 350F (175C). Lightly grease and lightly flour a 13" x 9" baking pan. In a large bowl, beat eggs until foamy. Add melted butter or margarine and mix well. Add BROWNIE MIX and blend well. Stir in vanilla. Stir in nuts and coconut. Pour into prepared pan. Bake about 30 mintues, until edges separate from pan. While still hot, carefully spread on marshmallow creme. Frost with Chocolate Icing. Makes 1 large cake.

Chocolate Icing

Put powdered sugar in a medium bowl. In a small saucepan, combine butter or margarine, evaporated milk and cocoa. Bring to a boil, stirring constantly. Remove from heat. Immediately add to powdered sugar. Beat until smooth.

Tropic Macaroons

A South Seas adventure in cookies.

2 cups BASIC COOKIE MIX, page 19
2 egg yolks
1 (8-1/2-oz.) can crushed pineapple, drained
1-1/4 cups shredded coconut, more if desired
Maraschino cherries, for garnish

Preheat oven to 350F (175C). Lightly grease baking sheets. In a medium bowl, combine BASIC COOKIE MIX, egg yolks, pineapple and coconut. Stir until well-blended. Drop by teaspoonfuls onto prepared baking sheets. Top with maraschino cherries. Bake 12 to 15 minutes, until edges are golden. Makes 30 to 36 cookies.

Chocolate Chip Cookies

The rich flavor of chocolate chips in every bite.

3 cups BASIC COOKIE MIX,
   page 19
3 tablespoons milk, more if
   necessary
1 teaspoon vanilla extract
1 egg
1/2 cup nuts or coconut
1 cup chocolate chips or
   sugar-coated chocolate
   candies

Preheat oven to 375F (190C). Grease baking sheets. In a large bowl, combine BASIC COOKIE MIX, milk, vanilla and egg. Blend well. Stir in nuts or coconut and chocolate chips or candies. Drop by teaspoonfuls onto prepared baking sheets. Bake 10 to 15 minutes, until golden brown. Makes about 24 cookies.

Banana-Coconut Delights

Make these giant-size and serve for breakfast with a glass of milk.

2 cups BASIC COOKIE MIX,
   page 19
1 cup flaked coconut
1 medium banana, mashed
1 teaspoon vanilla extract
1 egg, beaten
1/2 cup chopped nuts
1/2 cup rolled oats

Preheat oven to 375F (190C). Lightly grease baking sheets. In a medium bowl, combine BASIC COOKIE MIX, coconut, banana, vanilla and egg. Beat well. Stir in chopped nuts and oats. Drop by teaspoonfuls onto prepared baking sheets. Bake 10 to 12 minutes, until edges are browned. Makes about 36 cookies.

Peanut Butter Cookies

A better peanut butter batter.

3 cups BASIC COOKIE MIX,
   page 19
1/4 cup brown sugar, firmly
   packed
1 teaspoon vanilla extract
2 eggs
1/2 cup chunky-style peanut
   butter

Preheat oven to 375F (190C). Lightly grease baking sheets. Combine all ingredients in a medium bowl. Blend well. Shape dough into 1-inch balls. Place on prepared baking sheets and flatten with fork tines. Bake 10 to 12 minutes, until edges are browned. Makes 30 to 36 cookies.

Variation
Peanut Butter and Jelly Cookies: On baking sheets, press thumb into center of balls. Do not flatten. Fill with grape jelly.

Blueberry Dessert

A delightfully different party dessert.

3 cups COOKIE CRUMB
  CRUST MIX, page 20
2 eggs
1 cup butter or margarine,
  softened
2 cups powdered sugar
2 (3-oz.) pkgs. cream cheese,
  softened
1 (11-oz.) can blueberry pie
  filling
1 cup whipping cream, whipped
1/2 cup chopped pecans

Press all but 2 tablespoons COOKIE CRUMB CRUST MIX onto the bottom of an 11" x 7" baking pan. In a medium bowl, cream together eggs, butter or margarine, powdered sugar and cream cheese until smooth. Spread over crumb layer. Spread blueberry pie filling evenly over top. Top with whipped cream and sprinkle with a mixture of remaining 2 tablespoons crumbs and pecans. Refrigerate at least 12 hours. Cut into squares. Makes 15 to 20 servings.

Banana Split Cake

And you thought banana splits were made from ice cream!

2 cups COOKIE CRUMB
  CRUST MIX, page 20, or
  GRAHAM CRACKER
  CRUST MIX, page 21
1/4 cup butter or margarine,
  melted
2 eggs
1 cup butter or margarine,
  softened
2 cups sifted powdered sugar
3 to 4 bananas
1 (15-1/4-oz.) can crushed
  pineapple, drained
1 (13-1/2-oz.) carton whipped
  topping, thawed, or 1 pint
  sweetened whipped cream
1/4 to 1/2 cup chopped nuts

In a medium bowl, combine COOKIE CRUMB CRUST MIX and 1/4 cup melted butter or margarine. Press into an un-buttered 13" x 9" pan. In a medium bowl, combine eggs, 1 cup butter or margarine and powdered sugar. Beat 10 to 15 minutes, until smooth. Spread over crust in pan. Slice bananas evenly over top of mixture. Spread crushed pineapple evenly over bananas. Top with whipped topping or whipped cream. Sprinkle with nuts. Refrigerate 3 to 4 hours. Makes about 12 servings.

Blueberry Dessert

Lemonade Ice Cream Dessert

A light and cool dessert to top off any meal.

3 cups COOKIE CRUMB
    CRUST MIX, page 20, or
    GRAHAM CRACKER
    CRUST MIX, page 21
1/2 gallon vanilla ice cream,
    softened
1 (6-oz.) can frozen lemonade
    concentrate, still frozen

Press 2 cups of the COOKIE CRUMB CRUST MIX or GRA-HAM CRACKER CRUST MIX into an 11" x 7" baking pan. Put softened ice cream and frozen lemonade concentrate in a large bowl. Beat with an electric mixer until well blended. Quickly spoon ice cream mixture into crumb-lined pan. Top with remaining 1 cup crumbs. Freeze. Slice and serve. Makes 15 to 20 servings.

Chocolate-Marshmallow Dessert

If you don't like almonds, use a plain chocolate bar.

Graham Cracker Pie and
    Dessert Crust, baked, page 21
32 large marshmallows
1 (8-oz.) almond chocolate bar
1/2 cup milk
1 cup whipping cream, whipped
1/4 teaspoon almond extract

Prepare Graham Cracker Pie and Dessert Crust in a 9-inch square baking pan; set aside. In top of a double boiler, com-bine marshmallows, chocolate bar and milk. Stir over sim-mering water until marshmallows and chocolate are melted. Set aside to cool. Fold in whipped cream and almond extract. Spread mixture evenly over crust in pan. Refrigerate 3 to 4 hours. Makes about 9 servings.

Lemon Light Dessert

This refreshing dessert goes well with a meat and potato meal.

Graham Cracker Pie and
    Dessert Crust, unbaked,
    page 21
3 eggs, beaten
6 tablespoons lemon juice
Grated peel of 1 lemon (about
    1-1/2 teaspoons)
3/4 cup sugar
1 (13-oz.) can evaporated milk,
    partially frozen

Prepare Graham Cracker Pie and Dessert Crust in 9-inch square baking pan; set aside. In top of a double boiler, com-bine eggs, lemon juice, lemon peel and sugar. Cook and stir over hot water until thickened. Cool on a rack. In a large bowl, whip chilled evaporated milk until thick. Fold into cooled lemon mixture. Spoon evenly over crust in pan. Re-frigerate 3 to 4 hours. To serve, cut in squares. Makes about 9 servings.

Our Favorite Cheesecake

Baked cheesecake has a creamier texture when a pan of water is placed in the oven together with the cheesecake while baking.

Graham Cracker Pie and
Dessert Crust, baked, page 21
4 (8-oz.) pkgs. cream cheese,
room temperature
1-1/2 cups sugar
4 eggs, beaten
4 teaspoons vanilla extract
2 teaspoons fresh lemon juice
2 teaspoons grated lemon peel
Sour Cream Topping, see below
1 (21-oz.) can cherry-pie filling,
if desired

Sour Cream Topping:
1 cup dairy sour cream
1/4 cup sugar
1 teaspoon vanilla extract

Prepare Graham Cracker Pie and Dessert Crust in spring-form pan as directed; set aside to cool. Preheat oven to 325F (165C). In a large bowl, beat together cream cheese, sugar, eggs, vanilla, lemon juice and lemon peel until very smooth. Set aside. Spoon cream cheese mixture into baked crust in springform pan. Place in preheated oven and bake 1 hour 15 minutes. Meanwhile, prepare Sour Cream Topping. Spread topping on cheesecake and continue to bake 7 to 10 more minutes or until topping is set. Cool on wire rack. When completely cool cover with plastic wrap and refrigerate at least 8 hours or up to 24 hours. To serve, remove pan side. Top cheesecake with cherry-pie filling, if desired. Makes about 15 servings.

Sour Cream Topping

In a small bowl, combine sour cream, sugar and vanilla. Blend well.

Chocolate-Peppermint Supreme

Use your food processor to crush the peppermint candy.

Graham Cracker Pie and
Dessert Crust, unbaked,
page 21
1/2 cup butter or margarine,
softened
1 cup powdered sugar
3 eggs, separated, room
temperature
1 (1-oz.) square unsweetened
chocolate, melted
1/2 cup chopped nuts
1 cup whipping cream
1 (3-oz.) pkg. hard peppermint
candy, crushed
1/2 cup miniature
marshmallows
1/2 cup chopped nuts
3/4 cup GRAHAM CRACKER
CRUST MIX, page 21

Prepare Graham Cracker Pie and Dessert Crust in an 8-inch square baking pan; set aside. In a medium bowl, cream butter or margarine and powdered sugar. Beat in egg yolks. Stir in melted chocolate and 1/2 cup nuts. In a medium bowl, beat egg whites until soft peaks form. Fold into chocolate mixture; set aside. Spoon chocolate mixture over crust. Refrigerate 1 hour. Whip cream until stiff peaks form. Fold in peppermint candy, marshmallows and 1/2 cup nuts. Spoon evenly over chilled chocolate mixture. Sprinkle with GRAHAM CRACKER CRUST MIX. Refrigerate at least 1 hour. Makes about 12 servings.

Metric Chart

Comparison to Metric Measure

When You Know	Symbol	Multiply By	To Find	Symbol
teaspoons	tsp	5.0	milliliters	ml
tablespoons	tbsp	15.0	milliliters	ml
fluid ounces	fl. oz.	30.0	milliliters	ml
cups	c	0.24	liters	l
pints	pt.	0.47	liters	l

When You Know	Symbol	Multiply By	To Find	Symbol
quarts	qt.	0.95	liters	l
ounces	oz.	28.0	grams	g
pounds	lb.	0.45	kilograms	kg
Fahrenheit	F	5/9 (after subtracting 32)	Celsius	C

Liquid Measure to Liters

1/4 cup	=	0.06 liters
1/2 cup	=	0.12 liters
3/4 cup	=	0.18 liters
1 cup	=	0.24 liters
1-1/4 cups	=	0.3 liters
1-1/2 cups	=	0.36 liters
2 cups	=	0.48 liters
2-1/2 cups	=	0.6 liters
3 cups	=	0.72 liters
3-1/2 cups	=	0.84 liters
4 cups	=	0.96 liters
4-1/2 cups	=	1.08 liters
5 cups	=	1.2 liters
5-1/2 cups	=	1.32 liters

Liquid Measure to Milliliters

1/4 teaspoon	=	1.25 milliliters
1/2 teaspoon	=	2.5 milliliters
3/4 teaspoon	=	3.75 milliliters
1 teaspoon	=	5.0 milliliters
1-1/4 teaspoons	=	6.25 milliliters
1-1/2 teaspoons	=	7.5 milliliters
1-3/4 teaspoons	=	8.75 milliliters
2 teaspoons	=	10.0 milliliters
1 tablespoon	=	15.0 milliliters
2 tablespoons	=	30.0 milliliters

Fahrenheit to Celsius

F	C
200—205	95
220—225	105
245—250	120
275	135
300—305	150
325—330	165
345—350	175
370—375	190
400—405	205
425—430	220
445—450	230
470—475	245
500	260

INDEX